# alohacuisine

## Cookbooks by Sam Choy

### Mutual Publishing

*A Hawaiian Lū'au: Recipes, Music, and Talk Story*

*Sam Choy Woks the Wok: Stir-fry Cooking at Its Island Best*

*Sam Choy's Cooking with Kids*

*Sam Choy's Cooking—Island Cuisine at Its Best*

*Sam Choy's Kitchen: Cooking Doesn't Get Any Easier Than This!*

*Sam Choy's Little Hawaiian Cookbook for Big Appetites*

*Sam Choy's Little Hawaiian Poke Cookbook*

*Sam Choy's Sampler*

*The Choy of Seafood—Sam Choy's Pacific Harvest*

*With Sam Choy—Cooking From the Heart*

### Other

*Sam Choy's Cuisine Hawai'i*

*Sam Choy's Island Flavors*

*Sam Choy's Polynesian Kitchen*

# alohacuisine

## Chef Sam Choy

Mutual Publishing

Copyright © 2006 by Mutual Publishing

ISBN-10: 1-56647-799-9
ISBN-13: 978-1-56647-799-4

Library of Congress Cataloging-in-Publication Data

Choy, Sam.
Aloha cuisine / Sam Choy.
p. cm.
Summary: "Chef Sam Choy presents the best recipes of his signature
local fare from pupu to desserts"--Provided by publisher.
Includes index.
ISBN-13: 978-1-56647-799-4 (hardcover : alk. paper)
ISBN-10: 1-56647-799-9 (hardcover : alk. paper)
1. Hawaiian cookery. I. Title.
TX724.5.H3C45 2006
641.5'996--dc22
                                    2006020421

Design by Nancy Watanabe
Photos by Douglas Peebles except:
pages 6, 18, 22, 41, 56, 71, 90, 101, 105, 128, 130, 133 by Rae Huo
page 24 and 27 by Kaz Tanabe

First Printing, October 2006
1 2 3 4 5 6 7 8 9

Mutual Publishing, LLC
1215 Center Street, Suite 210
Honolulu, Hawaii 96816
Ph: (808) 732-1709
Fax: (808) 734-4094
email: info@mutualpublishing.com
www.mutualpublishing.com

Printed in Korea

# contents

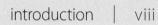

# introduction

I'm always asked to define my cuisine and it's always difficult for me to give a definitive answer. My cooking is an ongoing process that began long ago when I started to help my father prepare the lūʻau at Hukilau Beach in Lāʻie, Oʻahu where I grew up. (Then, cooking was a chore as I would have much rather been surfing with my friends.) As I travel to other parts of the US and other countries, I'm always watching how cooking is done elsewhere. Exciting culinary developments are taking place almost daily and I'm always eager to see what may work in Hawaiʻi.

I call my cooking Hawaiʻi Regional because it's about what we like to eat in Hawaiʻi, and it's only found here. Hawaiʻi is a place known worldwide as having some of the best food anywhere. I say this not because of hometown pride but because it is true. Lifelong exposure to culinary variety has made Hawaiʻi's people very knowledgeable about food. By virtue of our cultural heritage, local taste buds are very sophisticated. People here really know the difference between what is good food and what isn't. They are really advanced as far as food is concerned and always want to taste the latest and best (as well as the good old comfort food).

My cooking is about using the best and freshest ingredients of the islands. Fishermen still go out everyday to catch fish and small farmers grow exotic produce. Fresh food has always been served in the islands and it is the basis of the good food found here in fine dining rooms, ethnic restaurants, hole-in-the-wall eateries, lunch wagons, and at barbecues, lū'au, potlucks, and family gatherings.

My cuisine reflects the multi-ethnic nature of the islands. Hawai'i's multi-cultural society has been putting a large variety of foods into the island pot for decades. The melting pot began with the food that the Hawaiians ate and continued with the shared plantation field lunches, where there were exchanges of food ideas between ethnic groups. Local cuisine reflects diversity—raw fish, fresh seaweed, and tropical fruits of the Native Hawaiians; the star anise, fermented black beans, and steamed fish of the Chinese; the sashimi, tofu, and teriyaki of the Japanese; the sausage and sweet bread of the Portuguese.

My cuisine is about keeping recipes simple because I sense that people crave the simplicity and familiarity of food that

they have grown up with. But it's important to add a twist to make the dish. Above all make the meal memorable.

Presentation—an eye for color, how the food looks when served—is also an integral part of my cuisine. If people aren't turned on when they see it, then the recipe has failed. Decorate the dish, make it beautiful with edible flowers scattered on top or put little bow ties of green onion around the potatoes. The extra minute or two that the decorating takes can turn a dinner into a feast.

Most importantly my cuisine is about surprises that come from blending taste and flavors in unexpected ways. It's long on experimenting and trying to be different. It's short on doing the same thing forever. It's respectful of tradition but fueled forward by innovation. It's not afraid to be different, and it's understanding how taste and flavors seemingly different can harmonize.

I also strongly believe the recipes should be easy and fast to make both in the restaurant and at home. (I am not a fan of four-step cooking although it can taste good.) Island life has casualness to it that should be carried forward into cooking. I believe the magic lies in keeping things simple. When you start with the freshest island ingredients possible, little is left to make them better.

And last my cuisine is about love—aloha. Food in the islands has always been associated with caring and giving—from the feasts and lū'au of the early Hawaiians to the sharing of kau kau around the plantation lunch kettle that built bridges for people of different backgrounds to better understand each other.

So, in summary, here is what my cuisine is about —dishes reflecting the cooking of many ethnic backgrounds, relatively easy to make, utilizing fresh ingredients, and surprising taste and flavors used in unexpected ways.

Enjoy this collection of recipes that reflect my cooking. I call it Aloha Cuisine—food made from the heart and served always with pride and joy.

# pūpū

# Crab and Shrimp Stuffed Shiitake Mushrooms with Béarnaise Sauce

Fresh shiitake is the best mushroom in the world. The sweetness of the crab and shrimp melds well with the subtle flavor of the mushroom. While Béarnaise Sauce adds a rich and a creamy finish to this dish, you can top it off with any sauce.

Serves 16

16 large fresh shiitake mushrooms (about 1 pound)

1 cup heavy cream

1/2 cup chopped fresh spinach (or frozen chopped spinach, thawed and squeezed dry)

2 tablespoons chopped shallots

1/2 cup coconut milk

1 cup Ritz cracker crumbs

3/4 cup cooked Dungeness or other crabmeat

1/4 cup shrimp meat

1/4 teaspoon salt

1/4 teaspoon black pepper

Pinch fresh dill

3 tablespoons Parmesan cheese, grated

**Mango Béarnaise Sauce:**

1 tablespoon canola oil

3/4 cup butter (1 tablespoon plus 11 tablespoons)

2 shallots, peeled and finely chopped

2 or 3 sprigs fresh tarragon, chopped

2 sprigs fresh parsley, chopped

1/2 cup fresh mango, diced

2/3 cup vinegar

Salt and pepper to taste

3 egg yolks at room temperature

2 tablespoons cold water

Preheat oven to 350 degrees. Remove stems from shiitake mushrooms.

**Crab-shrimp mixture:** In a saucepan over medium-low heat, cook cream and spinach until reduced by half. Stir in shallots and cook 1 minute. Remove from heat and stir in coconut milk, cracker crumbs, crab, shrimp, salt, pepper, and dill. Stuff mushroom caps with crab-shrimp mixture. Place caps in a shallow baking pan. Put 1/2 tablespoon Mango Béarnaise Sauce on each stuffed mushroom. Bake 8 to 10 minutes. Sprinkle tops with Parmesan cheese.

**Mango Béarnaise Sauce — To make vinegar reduction:** In a saucepan, heat oil and 1 tablespoon butter. Add shallots, half of the tarragon, half of the parsley, 1/4 cup of the mango, vinegar, and pepper. Cook over gentle heat 20 minutes or until only 1 tablespoon liquid remains.

**To clarify butter:** In a bowl standing over a pan of hot water, melt remaining (11 tablespoons) butter. After several moments, milk solids will settle on bottom of pan. Pour off clear butter into another bowl, leaving milky residue behind.

**To finish Béarnaise:** In a bowl standing over a pan of hot water, combine egg yolks and vinegar reduction; whisk well. Gradually incorporate cold water, salt, and pepper, continuing to whisk vigorously until mixture becomes creamy. Remove bowl from heat and continue whisking, adding melted butter in a thin stream to make a very smooth sauce. Stir remaining tarragon, parsley, and mango into mixture. Use Béarnaise immediately or reserve in a bowl standing over a pan of hot, but not boiling, water.

# Deep-Fried Won Ton Brie
## with Fresh Pineapple Marmalade

This is a local alternative for those who enjoy cheese with bread, crackers, and fruit. This recipe has all the elements: the Brie cheese, the won ton wrappers, and the marmalade. The twist is the crispiness of the won ton.

Serving amount varies

**Won ton wrappers**
**Brie cheese**
**Oil for deep-frying**
**Pineapple Marmalade (see recipe below)**
**Macadamia or other nuts, optional**

**Pineapple Marmalade:**
**2 cups fresh or canned pineapple, chopped**
**1 cup granulated sugar**
**Pinch of hot chili pepper flakes, optional**

Take a won ton wrapper and brush with egg white. Place a cube of brie in the middle. (You can add a sprinkle of chopped macadamia nuts or other nuts, if you like.) Press the cheese down while gathering up the won ton wrapper to make a little purse, and pinch the wrapper together just above the cheese to seal. The won ton wrapper should fan out a little at the top to look like a miniature gift-wrapped package.

In a deep heavy pot or wok, heat oil to 350 degrees. Deep-fry purse to a golden brown for about 2 to 3 minutes. Drain on paper towels. Serve with warm pineapple marmalade.

**Variation:** Wrap the brie in phyllo dough and bake at 350 degrees for about 10 minutes or until golden brown.

**Pineapple Marmalade:** In a heavy saucepan, combine pineapple with sugar. Bring the mixture to a boil and then simmer, uncovered, until it thickens to a syrupy consistency, stirring occasionally. It will take about 45 minutes for fresh pineapple or less, if you're using canned pineapple.

**Tip:** For a quick dipping sauce, combine a jar of prepared orange or pineapple marmalade and thin with white wine over low heat for about 5 minutes or until the sauce becomes a good consistency for dipping. Spice it up with a pinch of hot chili pepper flakes.

Rae Huo

# Jumping Barbecue Shrimp
# with Mango Chutney

Shrimp and prawns are easy to prepare and fairly inexpensive compared to lobster. The only difference between shrimp and prawns is that prawns are fresh water while shrimp are salt water. Larger shrimps are easier to peel and devein.

**Serves 4**

**1 pound jumbo shrimp (16/20 count)**

**1/3 cup oil**

**2 tablespoons soy sauce**

**2 tablespoons cilantro, chopped**

**2 tablespoons ginger, minced**

**1 tablespoon garlic, minced**

**1 tablespoon lemon juice**

**1-1/2 teaspoons sugar**

**1/8 teaspoon crushed red pepper or 1 Hawaiian chili pepper, seeded and chopped**

**Mango chutney**

To prepare the shrimp:

Rinse shrimp and cut through the top shell but not all the way through the shrimp. Peel shell from shrimp, leaving shell and tail attached at tail. Devein shrimp.

Combine all remaining ingredients except mango chutney. Pour over shrimp and marinate for 30 minutes.

Place shrimp on barbecue or under broiler and cook three inches from heat for 3 to 5 minutes, turning once.

Serve with mango chutney.

# Ono Carpaccio
# with Hot Ginger Pepper Oil

This recipe developed when I experimented by adding ginger pesto to sashimi. The combination resulted in a sweet, fresh medley of flavors. I added a bit of kick with spicy oil on top.

**Serves 4**

**1-pound block very fresh ono (wahoo) fillet**

**Hot Ginger-Pepper Oil:**
**1/2 cup canola oil**
**1/4 teaspoon salt**
**1/4 cup ginger, minced**
**1/4 cup shallots, minced**
**1/4 cup lightly packed cilantro, minced**
**1/2 teaspoon red chili pepper flakes**
**1/8 teaspoon white pepper**

To prepare Hot Ginger-Pepper Oil:

Heat oil in a small saucepan. Add salt and cook 2 or 3 minutes. Stir in ginger, shallots, cilantro, chili pepper flakes, salt, and white pepper.

**Cut raw fish** in thin slices of desired size; 2-1/2 x 1-3/4 x 1/4 –inch is a suggested size.

Arrange fish slices attractively on a plate. A small circular dish of cubed tomatoes adds a nice touch.

Spoon Hot Ginger-Pepper Oil over fish.

# Yellowfin Tuna
# with Lime-Soy Sauce Marinade

Grilling is all about the charcoal. Each charcoal brings out a different taste of the food. In Hawai'i we love kiawe (algarroba) wood. The flavor of its smoke is very strong, like mesquite. It will send this dish into orbit.

Serves 4

4 (6-ounce) yellowfin 'ahi (yellowfin tuna) fillets

**Lime-Soy Sauce Marinade:**

1/4 cup soy sauce

1/4 cup canola oil

Juice and grated zest of 1 lime

2 tablespoons dry sherry

2 tablespoons cilantro, chopped

1 tablespoon garlic, minced

1 tablespoon brown sugar

2 teaspoons fresh ginger, minced

1/8 teaspoon Chinese five-spice powder

To prepare the marinade:

Combine all ingredients and mix well. Marinate fish for 1 hour, turning occasionally.

**Grill or broil fish** 10 to 12 minutes, turning once and basting occasionally with marinade. Do not overcook.

# Guava Barbecued Shrimp

Guavas are tart, high in Vitamin C, and most often used in jams and jellies. This recipe benefits from their tartness balancing the sweetness of the shrimp. Try a sauce made with puréed guavas on meat or duck as well, if you want to experiment the Sam Choy way.

**Serves 4**

**1 pound shrimp (16/20 count)**
**1/2 cup frozen guava concentrate, thawed**
**1/2 tablespoon honey**
**1 tablespoon soy sauce**
**1 teaspoon ginger, minced**
**1 tablespoon brown sugar**
**1 tablespoon basil, minced**

**To prepare the shrimp:**

Rinse shrimp and cut through the top shell but not all the way through the shrimp. Peel shell from shrimp, leaving shell and tail attached at tail. Devein shrimp.

**To prepare the marinade:**

In a mixing bowl, combine guava concentrate, honey, soy sauce, ginger, sugar, and basil; blend well. Add shrimp and marinate for 1 hour.

Skewer shrimp on four skewers. Barbecue or broil for 3 to 5 minutes, or until shrimp are cooked. Baste occasionally with marinade.

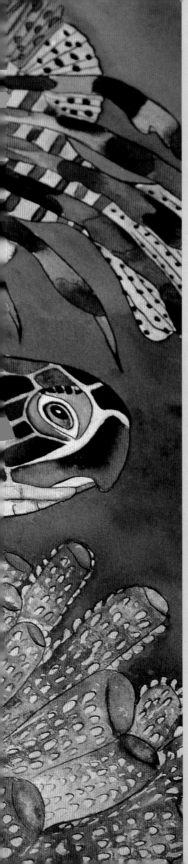

# salads

New Wave Marinated 'Ahi Salad | 17

Breadfruit, Sweet Potato, and Crabmeat Salad | 19

Macadamia Nut-Crusted Ono Caesar Salad | 20

Nineties Style Potato Salad | 23

Fried Shrimp and Calamari Salad | 25

Shrimp and Spinach Salad with Mango Vinaigrette | 26

# New Wave Marinated 'Ahi Salad

Contrasting tastes and textures — cold with warm, crisp with firm — make this salad fun to eat. Each layer has a new and wonderful flavor. Together they work in harmony. The tortilla cup adds crunch.

Serves 1 to 2

2 to 3 ounces dry Japanese soba or
    somen noodles

Salad greens

Salad dressing of your choice

1 flour tortilla

Oil for deep-frying

3 'ahi (yellowfin tuna) fillets
    (2 ounces each and about 1/2-inch
    thick)

1 tablespoon olive oil

**New Wave Marinade:**

1/2 cup soy sauce

1/4 cup light salad oil

2 tablespoons mirin
    (Japanese sweet rice wine)

1/4 teaspoon sesame oil

1/2 tablespoon fresh cilantro, minced

2 tablespoons green onion, thinly
    sliced

1 tablespoon fresh garlic, minced

1 tablespoon fresh ginger,
    peeled and minced

1/2 teaspoon salt

1/4 teaspoon white pepper

1-1/2 teaspoons brown sugar

1/2 teaspoon ground Chinese
    five-spice powder

1 tablespoon black sesame seeds

Pinch of dried red chili pepper flakes
    or 1 fresh Hawaiian chili pepper

**Make the New Wave Marinade:** Combine marinade ingredients and stir until sugar dissolves.

**Cook and marinate the noodles:** Cook the soba or somen according to package directions. Rinse well in cold water and drain. Mix 2 to 4 tablespoons of New Wave Marinade with noodles and chill for at least 20 to 30 minutes.

**Prepare Garnish:** Carrot, beet, and radish curls, or grated carrots and zucchini

3 cucumber slices

3 tomato wedges

Sprig of fresh cilantro

Sprinkle of black sesame seeds, Macadamia nuts or walnuts, chopped

Assemble ingredients and set aside while you prepare the fish and the tortilla.

**Marinate and cook the 'ahi:** Marinate the 'ahi for 5 minutes; set it aside for a few minutes while you deep-fry the tortilla until golden brown. Drain tortilla on paper towels. Heat the olive oil on a flat griddle or in a sauté pan and sear the 'ahi on both sides, about 1 minute per side. (You want the fish to remain raw in the middle.)

**Assemble the dish:** Place tortilla on a salad plate and add a handful or two of your favorite greens broken into bite-size pieces. Place the cold noodles on top of the greens, then arrange warm fish on top. Place your vegetable curls or grated vegetable garnish on top of the fish, add a sprig of cilantro, and sprinkle with black sesame seeds or chopped nuts. Place the cucumber slices and tomato wedges around the edge of the plate and serve with Creamy Oriental Dressing (see p. 34) or your favorite dressing.

Rae Huo

# Breadfruit, Sweet Potato, and Crabmeat Salad

Breadfruit trees were brought to Hawai'i from Tahiti. The fruit can weigh over 10 pounds and has a warty rind. It turns yellow-green when mature and is sweet when ripe. Irish or baking potatoes can be substituted for breadfruit.

**Serves 12**

**1 small breadfruit**
**2 medium sweet potatoes**
**1 cup carrots, julienne**
**1/2 cup celery, thinly sliced**
**2 cups shredded crabmeat**
**3 hard-boiled eggs, chopped**
**1/2 cup onion, thinly sliced**
**1-1/2 cups mayonnaise**
**Salt and pepper to taste**

Peel breadfruit and sweet potatoes; cut into 1-inch cubes. Cook in lightly salted boiling water until fork-tender. Set aside to cool.

Blanch carrots and celery.

In a large mixing bowl combine breadfruit, sweet potatoes, carrots, celery, crabmeat, eggs, onion, and mayonnaise; toss lightly. Season to taste with salt and pepper.

# Macadamia Nut-Crusted Ono Caesar Salad

Caesar salad can become a meal all by itself, depending on what is added. To serve this salad, place romaine lettuce leaves in a salad bowl and toss with dressing. Divide the lettuce among the four plates, place a fish fillet atop each salad, and garnish with freshly ground black pepper, croutons, and Parmesan cheese. Striped marlin or 'ahi, raw or seared, can also be substituted.

Serves 4

**2 medium heads romaine lettuce, washed, dried, and torn**

**Caesar Salad Dressing (see recipe to right)**

**2 Macadamia Nut-Crusted Ono (wahoo) (see recipe below)**

**Macadamia Nut-Crusted Ono:**

**4 (6-ounce) ono (wahoo) fillets**

**1/8 cup light olive oil**

**1 teaspoon fresh ginger, minced**

**1 teaspoon fresh garlic, minced**

**Salt and pepper to taste**

**1/4 cup panko (Japanese-style crispy breadcrumbs)**

**1/4 cup butter, at room temperature**

**1/4 cup macadamia nuts, chopped**

**1/2 teaspoon fresh basil, minced**

**1/2 teaspoon fresh dill, minced**

**1/2 teaspoon fresh thyme, minced**

**1/2 teaspoon paprika**

**Garnish:**

**Freshly ground black pepper to taste**

**Croutons**

**1/4 cup Parmesan cheese, freshly grated**

## Macadamia Nut-Crusted Ono:

Marinate ono for 1 hour in the olive oil, ginger, garlic, salt, and pepper. Preheat oven to 375 degrees. Combine panko, butter, macadamia nuts, herbs, and paprika; blend well. Press marinated fish into panko mixture, and bake for 8 to 10 minutes.

## Caesar Salad Dressing:

| | |
|---|---|
| 1 egg yolk | 2 teaspoons Worcestershire sauce |
| 1 tablespoon Dijon mustard | 2 tablespoons red wine vinegar |
| 1 teaspoon fresh lemon juice | 2 tablespoons Parmesan cheese |
| 2 cloves fresh garlic, minced | 1/4 cup water |
| 1 tablespoon anchovies, minced | Salt and pepper to taste |
| Dash Tabasco® sauce | 1-1/2 cups salad oil |

Whisk egg yolk until creamy. Add remaining ingredients (except the oil) and blend well. Slowly drizzle in the oil, whisking constantly until oil is homogenized and dressing is creamy. This may also be done in a blender. The secret is to add the oil slowly so that the mixture gels rather than separates. Chill.

## Final preparation:

Place romaine lettuce leaves in a salad bowl and toss with dressing. Divide the lettuce among four plates, place one fish fillet atop each salad, and garnish with freshly ground black pepper, croutons, and Parmesan cheese.

Rae Huo

# Nineties Style Potato Salad

There are different textures and flavors in this salad—the sweetness of the crab, the crunchiness of corn kernels. Low-starch Red Bliss Potatoes are the potato of choice for salads as they stay firm when cut.

**Serves 18 (1/2-cup servings)**

**2 pounds new Red Bliss (round red boiling) potatoes**
**2 cups shredded crabmeat**
**1/2 cup bay shrimps**
**4 hard-boiled eggs, chopped**
**1 cup fresh corn kernels**
**1/2 cup pitted medium black olives**
**1/4 cup sliced water chestnuts**
**1-1/2 cups fresh spinach, chopped**
**1/2 cup Maui onion, minced**
**1/2 cup celery, minced**
**1/2 cup carrots, grated**
**2-1/2 cups mayonnaise**
**Salt and pepper to taste**

Peel then cook potatoes in lightly salted boiling water until fork-tender. Cool, then cut into eighths.

In a large mixing bowl, toss all ingredients lightly to combine. Adjust seasoning with salt and pepper, if necessary.

Kaz Tanabe

# Fried Shrimp and Calamari Salad

The paprika-spiced calamari rings together with the shrimp result in a wonderful, crunchy texture. Maui onions are noted for their mild, spicy flavor (Spanish onions can be substituted). For quick cooking, choose smaller squid with clear eyes and moist flesh, as they are more tender. Their aroma should be like the ocean with no strong, fishy smell. Cover tightly and refrigerate in the coldest refrigerator section or on a bed of ice. Fresh squid should be used within two days or cleaned and frozen immediately for later use. Squid is most abundant during spring and summer.

Serves 6–8

Oil for deep-frying

2 cups flour

1 tablespoons paprika

1 pound calamari, cleaned and cut into rings

1 pound shrimp (21/25 count)

Salt and pepper to taste

1 pound salad greens

1/2 red bell pepper, julienne

1/2 yellow bell pepper, julienne

1/2 medium Maui onion, julienne

1 medium cucumber, peeled, seeded, and sliced

2 medium tomatoes, cut into wedges

Kaiware sprouts (daikon radish sprouts), for garnish

Pickled Ginger Vinaigrette (see recipe below)


**Pickled Ginger Vinaigrette:**

4 teaspoons dashi (fish broth)

2-1/2 cups sugar

1 cup rice wine vinegar

12 ounces pickled ginger

3 tablespoons fresh ginger

Pinch of salt

1-1/2 cups salad oil

Heat the oil to 350 degrees. Combine the flour and paprika. Moderately season the calamari and shrimp with salt and pepper. Add calamari and shrimp to the flour mixture. Remove, and dust off the excess flour. Deep-fry the calamari and shrimp until golden brown.

Arrange the salad greens, peppers, onion, cucumber, and tomatoes on a platter. Place the calamari and shrimp on the top and garnish with kaiware sprouts. Serve with Pickled Ginger Vinaigrette.

Pickled Ginger Vinaigrette:
In a mixing bowl, combine dashi with sugar and rice wine vinegar. Transfer mixture to a blender and add fresh ginger, pickled ginger, and pinch of salt. Slowly add salad oil to the blender. Serve chilled.

# Shrimp and Spinach Salad
# with Mango Vinaigrette

There are three basic types of spinach. Savoy spinach, sold in fresh bunches, has crinkly, curly leaves with a dark green color. Springy and crisp, it's particularly good in salads. Flat or smooth-leaf spinach has unwrinkled, spade-shaped leaves that are easier to clean than Savoy; it is mostly used for canned and frozen spinach as well as soups, baby foods, and other processed foods. Semi-savoy spinach, becoming increasingly popular, has slightly crinkled leaves. Cultivated for both the fresh market and for processing, it offers some of the texture of Savoy, but is not as difficult to clean.

Serves 8–10

1 tablespoon garlic, minced

salt and pepper to taste

olive oil

1 pound shrimp (21/25 count), peeled
    and deveined

1 pound scallops (U-10 size)

2 pounds fresh spinach

1-1/2 cups fresh hearts of palm, julienne

1 medium red onion, julienne

Mango Vinaigrette (see recipe on right)

Fresh mango slices

### Shrimp and Scallops:

Sauté garlic in olive oil and add shrimp. Sear one minute on each side. Season with salt and pepper to taste.

Season scallops with salt and pepper to taste. Sear in a pan with oil for one minute on each side until lightly brown in color.

Thoroughly wash spinach leaves. Tear leaves into bite-size pieces and place in a large salad bowl. Add shrimp, scallops, hearts of palm, onion, and desired amount of dressing. Toss until salad is well-coated. Top with mango slices.

### Mango Vinaigrette:

| | |
|---|---|
| 1/4 cup apple cider vinegar | 1 tablespoon fresh basil, chopped |
| 1/2 cup mango purée | 1 clove garlic, minced |
| 1 teaspoon Dijon mustard | Salt and pepper, to taste |
| 2 tablespoons sugar | 1/2 cup canola oil |

Combine all ingredients except oil. Whisk until sugar is completely dissolved and mixture is thoroughly blended. Gradually add oil while continuing to whisk. Chill before using.

Kaz Tanabe

# poke

# Spicy Poke

Poke, the cubed raw fish in this traditional Hawaiian dish, is seasoned and marinated by the soy sauce, sesame oil, and additional ingredients. It works well as an appetizer or as a main dish when seared and served over rice. Depending on how much chili pepper is used, accompany with an icy drink, rice, or a cool bowl of fresh poi. The limu is crunchy, the 'ahi is firm, and the rest is just right.

Serves 4 to 6

1 pound fresh 'ahi (yellowfin tuna),
    1/2-inch pieces

1 medium tomato, diced 1/4-inch pieces

1 cup limu (seaweed), chopped ( Substitute
    with dehydrated wakame or hijiki, available
    in most grocery stores. Before using, soak
    in water to cover for 10-15 minutes.)

1/2 cup round onion, chopped

1 cup cucumber, diced 1/4-inch pieces

1/2 cup green onion, diced 1/4-inch pieces

2 tablespoons soy sauce

1 teaspoon sesame oil

1/2 teaspoon Hawaiian chili peppers, crushed,
    seeded, and minced

1 teaspoon kim chee base

Salt and pepper to taste

In a mixing bowl, combine all ingredients. Toss gently. Be sure to keep the fish very cold. Add salt and pepper to taste.

# Poke Cakes

Poke has become an important part of Hawai'i Regional cuisine. Living in Hawai'i, you need to offer a variety of fish recipes. Poke cakes came about when I saw vendors selling surimi at an Asian market and later that day, having pork hash at a Chinese restaurant. I knew I would do something similar with 'ahi.

Serves 1–2

**Patties:**

1 cup fresh 'ahi (yellowfin tuna), 3/8-inch cubes

1/2 cup onion, minced

1/2 cup green onion, minced

1 egg

3 tablespoons soy sauce

2 tablespoons sesame oil

Salt and pepper to taste

**Coating:**

Panko (crispy Japanese-style bread crumbs)

4 tablespoons salad oil

2 tablespoons green onion, chopped for garnish

**Sauce:**

1/2 cup enoki mushrooms

4 tablespoons butter

2 teaspoons soy sauce

2 teaspoons oyster sauce

2 teaspoons cilantro, chopped

To prepare the patties:

Combine patty ingredients and form 6 patties. Press patties in panko to coat. In a frying pan, warm oil over medium-high heat. Gently place patties in pan and brown both sides, keeping the inside of the patties medium rare. Arrange on a platter, and garnish with green onion.

To prepare the sauce:

Sauté the mushrooms in butter for 2 minutes. Add remaining sauce ingredients and cook for another minute. Pour sauce over patties and serve.

# Sam Choy's Big Aloha Fried Poke Wrap

A south-of-the-border tortilla turns multi-ethnic when it's folded around fried rice, stir-fry poke, and topped with dressings. Sautéed chicken or beef can be substituted.

Serves 2 (multiply to increase serving)

5 ounces of fried poke (see recipe below)

2 (12-inch) flour tortillas

2 ounces shredded greens (about ¾ cup)

1 cup fried rice (see p. 117 Sam Choy's Island Lup Cheong Fried Rice)

4 tablespoons Sam Choy's Creamy Oriental Dressing (see recipe below)

4 tablespoons Wasabi Mayonnaise (see recipe below)

**Poke:**

4 to 6 ounces 'ahi, cut into ¾-inch cubes

1 teaspoon soy sauce

¼ cup round onion, chopped

1 teaspoon green onion

¼ cup ogo (seaweed)

1 teaspoon sesame oil

**Creamy Oriental Dressing:**

3 cups mayonnaise

½ cup soy sauce

¾ cup granulated sugar

¼ teaspoon white pepper

1 ½ tablespoons black sesame seeds

1 tablespoon sesame oil

Place 'ahi cubes in a mixing bowl and add remaining ingredients. Mix well, then quickly sear in 1 tablespoon of hot oil on high heat in a wok. Don't cook for more than a minute or two, as you want the center raw.

Lightly heat tortillas one at a time over wok.

Layer half of the shredded greens, fried rice, and poke onto each tortilla wrap. Top with Creamy Oriental Dressing and Wasabi Mayonnaise to taste. Roll tortilla wraps and eat.

Variation:

Use taro flavored or spinach tortillas.

Creamy Oriental Dressing:

Place all ingredients in a medium-size bowl and whisk together until well blended. If necessary, whisk in a few drops of water at a time until you get the consistency you want. Refrigerate until used.

Wasabi Mayonnaise:

Make a paste of the wasabi powder and water. Whisk into mayonnaise until completely mixed. Season with a pinch of salt and black pepper. Refrigerate.

**Wasabi Mayonnaise:**

1 tablespoon wasabi powder

2 tablespoons water

½ cup mayonnaise

Salt and pepper to taste

# soups

# Da Wife's Bean Soup

At family gatherings, it's the wife's soup or mine. My soup always has leftovers; her soup is always gone. (I think we eat more to make her feel better!—Just kidding.) Some argue that fresh dried beans do not benefit from pre-soaking before cooking. Heating the legumes to boiling and then simmering until they swell with water and soften can be done in one continuous process. Soaking the beans removes only 5-10 percent of the gas-producing sugars that can cause digestive problems for some people. Nevertheless, I prefer overnight soaking.

Serves 18

**2 cups dried beans (kidney, pinto, or small red)**
**2 smoked ham hocks or ham shanks**
**3 cups chicken stock**
**1 cup cilantro, chopped**
**2 cups potato, diced**
**2 cups carrots, diced**
**1-1/2 cups onion, diced**
**1/2 cup celery, diced**
**1 Portuguese sausage (10 ounces)**
**2 cups tomato purée**
**Salt and pepper to taste**

**To prepare the dried beans:**
Soak beans in water overnight. Drain.

**To prepare the soup:**
In a stockpot, combine soaked beans, ham hocks, chicken stock, cilantro, and water to cover (about 6 cups). Bring to a boil, then simmer until meat and beans are tender, about 1 to 1-1/2 hours.

Remove skin and bones from ham hocks; shred meat and return to stock.

Slice and fry Portuguese sausage, and blot with paper towel. Add sausage to stockpot along with potatoes, carrots, onion, celery, and tomato purée. Cook until potatoes are tender. Season with salt and pepper.

Goes great with freshly baked bread.

# Tahitian Crabmeat Soup

In Hawai'i, crabs come in many shapes, colors, and sizes, depending on where they live. Live crabs should be covered in a brine solution (1/3 cup salt, one gallon of water) for thirty minutes so that they can naturally filter themselves clean. Prepare as quickly as possible so they're fresh when they arrive on the dining room table.

Serves 8

2 cups onion, diced
1/4 cup butter
2 tablespoons flour
2 cups heavy cream
1-1/2 cups chicken stock
2 cups coconut milk
2 cups frozen chopped spinach, thawed, or 3 cups chopped fresh spinach, washed and stemmed
1-1/2 cups crabmeat
Salt and white pepper to taste

In a large saucepan sauté onion in butter until translucent.

Stir in flour; blend well. Add heavy cream and chicken stock; simmer for 5 minutes, stirring frequently.

Stir in coconut milk, spinach, and crabmeat. Cook for 3 minutes, stirring frequently. Season to taste with salt and white pepper.

# Taro Corm Chowder

This is one of my favorite soups. Taro is what they make poi out of. Some people think eating poi is like eating wallpaper paste. But when I cook this chowder and sneak the taro in, you should see them go, "Oh, wow! What is this? It's so good!" I get a kick out of telling them it's taro. Taro corms have a subtle, nut-like flavor, are highly nutritious, and are an exceptional source of fiber and carbohydrates. Corms can be pan-fried, deep-fried, baked, roasted, broiled, mashed, sliced, or steamed, and go well with any meat dish, soup, or stew. If taro is not available, substitute Russet or Red Bliss potatoes.

Serves 8 to 10

**2 lbs. taro, diced small**
**3/4 cup salt pork or bacon**
**3/4 cup onions, diced small**
**3/4 cup celery, diced small**
**1-1/2 cups flour**
**1 quart chicken stock**
**2 cups creamed corn**
**4 cups whole kernel corn**
**2 pints heavy cream**
**Salt and white pepper to taste**

**To prepare the taro:**
Place taro in pot, cover with water, bring to a boil, reduce heat, and simmer until tender, then set aside.

**To prepare the soup:**
Sauté bacon or chopped salt pork with onions and celery until onions are translucent. Add flour and stir until the oil in the pan moistens the flour completely and turns it into a paste, similar to what French cooks call a "blond roux." Whisk in chicken stock, creamed corn, whole kernel corn, taro, and heavy cream. Adjust seasoning with salt and pepper. Let simmer 6 to 8 minutes, then serve hot.

# Roasted Pumpkin Soup

Pumpkin is a round orange winter squash that's underrated. Most of the pumpkins sold in the United States are used as Halloween Jack-o-lanterns; that's a lot of good food wasted! Pumpkin is high in beta-carotene and fiber, and provides protein, complex carbohydrates, Vitamin C, and potassium. Pumpkin pie is one of my favorites, and in this recipe, pumpkin serves as the basis of a delicious soup.

## Serves

**1 pumpkin, 3 pounds**
**3 tablespoons butter**
**3 tablespoons minced garlic**
**1 cup onion, chopped**
**4 cups chicken stock**
**1/2 cup heavy cream**
**Salt and freshly cracked black pepper
  to taste**

## To prepare the pumpkin:

Peel and cut pumpkin into cubes. Season with olive oil and pepper. Place on a rimmed baking pan and add 1/4 inch water to the pan. Cover with foil and bake at 350°F for about 45 minutes or until tender.

**Sauté** butter, onion, and garlic. Add pumpkin and chicken stock. Bring to a boil and simmer for 30 minutes.

**Purée** soup in blender until smooth. Strain through a sieve into a clean pot. Add cream and season with salt and pepper.

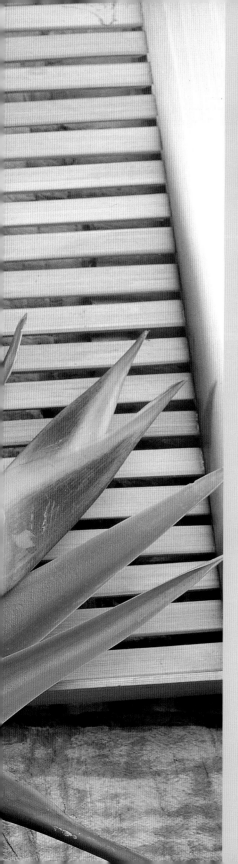

# poultry

# Chicken Hekka

Growing up, my family always made chicken hekka for mainland guests. This is a cornerstone recipe in my cookbook bible. This comfort food dish is light and tasty, just what's needed after a previous day's over-indulgence in rich food and drink.

**Serves 4-6**

2-1/2 pounds boneless chicken thighs or breasts

3 tablespoons oil

1 inch of fresh ginger, crushed

1 (No. 2) can sliced bamboo shoots

10 stalks green onion, cut in 1-inch lengths

1 medium carrot, julienne

1 pound shiitake mushrooms, sliced

2 stalks celery, julienne

1/2 pound watercress, cut into 1-inch lengths

1 bundle (2 ounces) bean threads, cooked and cut into 1-inch lengths

1/2 block tofu

**Sake Sauce:**

1/2 cup sugar

3/4 cup soy sauce

1/2 cup chicken broth

1/2 cup sake

Combine marinade ingredients and marinate chicken for 30 minutes.

## Marinade:

| | |
|---|---|
| 1/2 cup soy sauce | 1/2 teaspoon salt |
| 1/2 cup oil | 1/4 teaspoon white pepper |
| 2 tablespoons mirin | 2 tablespoons cornstarch |
| 1 tablespoon garlic, minced | 1-1/2 teaspoons brown sugar |
| 1 tablespoon ginger, minced | |

Slice vegetables, mix, and set aside.

## To prepare the Sake Sauce:

Blend ingredients and set aside.

## To assemble the dish:

Brown chicken in 3 tablespoons oil to which you have added crushed ginger. Add all vegetables and cook for 1 minute. Add Sake Sauce and bean threads and simmer on medium for 5 minutes.

Drain tofu, cut into bite-size cubes, and add to everything. Mix lightly, then remove from heat. Serve with hot rice.

# Hibachi Miso Chicken with Peanut Butter

The marinade melds traditional and modern flavors—miso and teriyaki with peanut butter and beer. Use either a Kamado or a barbecue with a cover to grill the fillets for 35 minutes, or first skewer and then grill. Miso paste is made from fermented soy beans and rice or barley. There are dozens of types but the most common are the white, red, and black miso.

**Serves 16**

**5 pounds boneless chicken thighs**

**Marinade:**
1/2 cup miso (fermented soybean paste)
1/2 cup smooth peanut butter
1/2 cup soy sauce
1/2 cup sugar
1/2 cup beer
2 tablespoons fresh ginger, minced
1 tablespoon garlic, minced

Combine marinade ingredients and marinate chicken overnight in refrigerator.

Grill over charcoal. Serve with hot rice.

# Macadamia Nut Chicken Breast

Macadamia nuts have a very hard shell. The nut is enclosed in a green husk that splits open as it matures. The seed coat is smooth when in the shell, holding a creamy white kernel containing up to 80 percent oil and 4 percent sugar. When roasted, it develops a uniform color and texture. Macadamia nuts were first introduced to Hawai'i from eastern Australia in the late 19th century. They were not grown commercially until the 1950s. We usually think of macadamia nuts as ingredients in sweets, candies, desserts, and pies. But these versatile nuts also work well in main dishes. I use chopped nuts as a crust in several recipes.

Serves 4

4 (6-ounce) boneless chicken breasts
3 whole eggs, whipped
1-1/2 cups panko (Japanese style breadcrumbs) or dry breadcrumbs
1 cup chopped macadamia nuts
2 tablespoons fresh parsley, chopped
1-1/2 cups all-purpose flour
1/2 cup olive oil

**Minted Pineapple-Papaya Marmalade:**
1/2 cup papaya, diced
1/2 cup pineapple, diced
3 tablespoons granulated sugar
Fresh chopped mint or spearmint

**Marinade:**
1 cup soy sauce
4 tablespoons brown sugar
1 tablespoon fresh ginger, peeled and minced
1 tablespoon fresh garlic, minced
1/2 cup sherry

To prepare the marmalade:
Combine papaya, pineapple, and sugar in a heavy saucepan. Simmer for 20 minutes stirring occasionally. Then add a pinch of fresh chopped mint or spearmint and stir. Set aside.

To prepare the marinade:
Combine all marinade ingredients and stir until sugar is dissolved. Marinate chicken for 30 to 45 minutes.

To cook the chicken:
Meanwhile, mix panko, macadamia nuts, and parsley. Remove chicken from marinade and blot off excess liquid. Dust chicken with flour; dip into whipped eggs and then press the panko-macadamia nut mixture firmly onto chicken.

Lightly coat frying pan with olive oil to cover bottom. Heat oil on medium-high and cook chicken 3 or 4 minutes on each side until golden brown. Don't overcook. Add more oil as needed.

Serve with Minted Pineapple-Papaya Marmalade as a dipping sauce.

# Sam Choy's Award-Winning Roast Duck

This "People's Award" winning dish is much easier to cook than it seems. This simple, short-cut recipe offers all the taste of a traditional Chinese roast duck in half the time. When shopping for a whole duck, look for a plump, firm duck breast without any noticeable wrinkles. Push a finger into the duck breast to check it for firmness. If the duck is frozen, you'll have to skip this test and just look for a plump breast and thighs.

Serves 4-6

2 (3- to 4-pound) ducks
3/4 cup soy sauce

**Dry Rub:**
1 tablespoon salt
1 tablespoon garlic salt
1 teaspoon garlic powder
1 teaspoon paprika
1/2 teaspoon white pepper
1 tablespoon coriander seeds (whole)

**To prepare the duck:**
Remove wing tips, neck flap, tail end, excess fat, and drumstick knuckles. Rinse both ducks. Place in a dish, and pour soy sauce over them. Roll the ducks in the soy sauce and marinate 20 minutes, turning the duck every 3 to 4 minutes.

Preheat oven to 550 degrees.

**To prepare the dry rub:**
Mix remaining ingredients to make a dry rub. Place duck breast right side up on a rack in a roasting pan and sprinkle thoroughly with dry rub. Also, put a little dry rub inside cavities.

Roast for 30 minutes. Reduce heat to 325 degrees. Cook for 1 hour or until meat thermometer registers an internal temperature of 170 to 175 degrees. No basting is necessary.

Serve with steamed rice.

# Sam's Original Shoyu Chicken

Soy sauce (frequently called shoyu in the islands) is made from soy beans, wheat, salt, and yeast. There are many varieties of shoyu available for purchase. The best varieties have rich, deep, complex flavors. Store them in a cool dark place or refrigerate them, and once opened, try to use them up, as soy sauce products are better when fresh.

Serves 6

**1-1/2 pounds chicken thighs**
**2 cups Basic Teriyaki Sauce**
  **(see recipe on p. 70 )**
**1/2 teaspoon Chinese five-spice powder**
**1 tablespoon cilantro, minced**
**1 tablespoon cornstarch**
**2 tablespoons water**

**Garnish:**
**Scallion brushes**

In a medium saucepan combine chicken, Teriyaki Sauce, Chinese five-spice powder, and cilantro. Bring to a boil and add chicken; reduce heat and simmer about 20 to 25 minutes, or until chicken is tender. Remove chicken from sauce; set aside and keep warm.

Blend cornstarch and water to make a smooth paste. Bring 1 cup of the sauce to a boil; stir in cornstarch mixture.

Reduce heat and simmer, stirring frequently, until thickened. Brush chicken with the glaze. Garnish with scallion brushes.

## Scallion brushes:
Trim scallion roots and remove the last few inches of the green stems, leaving about 2-1/2 inches of bulb and stems. Make crisscross cuts about 1/2 inch deep at both ends of each brush and spread the fringed ends gently. Put the scallions in a bowl of ice-water and chill them for 2 hours, or until the fringed ends have curled. Drain well.

# Spiced Roasted Chicken

When substituting dried herbs for fresh, remember that their strengths vary. The general rule is to use a generous ¼ teaspoon ground or 1 teaspoon of crumbled dry leaves for every tablespoon of the fresh herb finely chopped. The melding of spices with the heat of the chili flakes intensifies the flavor and the coloring of the chicken in this dish. The sweetness of the marmalade adds another layer of flavor.

Serves 6

1 (5-pound) roasting chicken, rinse and pat dry

**Rub:**
1 tablespoon roasted fennel seeds
1/2 teaspoon roasted cumin seeds
2 teaspoons ground turmeric
2 teaspoons chili flakes
1/4 cup cilantro leaves, chopped
1/4 cup scallions, chopped
4 cloves garlic
1-inch cube ginger, sliced
2 tablespoons soy sauce
Salt to taste

**Papaya Pineapple Marinade:**
1 small fresh pineapple, peeled, cored, and chopped
1 medium fresh papaya, seeded, peeled, and chopped
6 tablespoons sugar

**Asian Pilaf:**
1 cup basmati rice
1 cup water
1 tablespoon butter
2 tablespoons garlic, minced

To prepare the rub:

Grind the fennel, cumin, turmeric, and chili flakes in a coffee grinder. In a food processor, pulverize the ground spices, cilantro, scallions, garlic, and ginger. Add soy sauce and season with salt to taste.

Rub the mixture on the inside and outside of the chicken. Marinate chicken in the refrigerator for 2 to 3 hours. Preheat the oven to 300 degrees. Place chicken on a rack in a large roasting pan and roast for 2 hours or until done. Let rest for 10 minutes before carving. Serve on a bed of Asian Pilaf with Papaya Pineapple Marinade.

Papaya Pineapple Marinade:

In a medium saucepan, combine all ingredients. Cook over medium heat for 1 hour or until mixture has a syrupy consistency, stirring occasionally.

Asian Pilaf:

Combine all ingredients, bring to a boil, and simmer for 20 minutes.

# meats

The Best Beef Stew | 63

Hale'iwa Barbecued Pork Ribs | 65

Honomalino Lamb with Satay Sauce | 66

Ka'ū Mac Nut-Crusted Roast Loin of Pork with Tropical Marmalade | 69

Paniolo Steak | 70

Papa Choy's Beef Tomato | 73

Asian Braised Short Ribs | 75

# The Best Beef Stew

The natural flavors of the beef and vegetables make this a comfort food classic. The surprise combo of beef stock and chicken stock gives the gravy a smooth taste. This island favorite is thickened with mochiko, a flour milled from short-grain glutinous rice. Mochiko is also called mochi flour, sweet rice flour, or sweet glutinous rice flour. Mochiko is a good thickening agent because it creates a strong bond that withstands refrigerator and freezer temperatures without separating. Traditionally used to make Japanese desserts such as mochi and manju, here, it's used in a stew.

## Serves 6

4 pounds chuck roast

Salt and pepper to taste

All-purpose flour to dust meat (about 1 cup)

1/2 cup salad oil

2 cloves garlic, crushed

1 small onion, minced

1/2 cup celery leaves, chopped

5 cups beef stock or low-sodium broth

2 cups chicken broth

1-1/2 cups tomato paste

3 medium carrots, cut in 1-1/2-inch chunks

4 potatoes, cut in 1-1/2-inch chunks

2 medium onions, cut in 1-1/2-inch chunks

4 stalks celery, cut in 1-1/2-inch chunks

Mochiko (sweet rice flour) and water to thicken

Cut beef into bite-size pieces and sprinkle with salt and pepper. Dust beef with flour.

In a large pot, heat oil over medium heat and brown meat with garlic, onion, and celery leaves for about 10 minutes or until well-browned. Keep stirring to avoid burning.

Drain oil and add beef and chicken broth and tomato paste. Stir and bring mixture to a boil, then reduce heat to simmer. Cover and let cook about 1 hour, or until beef is tender.

Add carrots and potatoes and cook 5 minutes. Add onion chunks and celery and cook 10 minutes more. Adjust seasoning with salt and pepper.

Mix mochiko and water into a thick syrup. Bring stew to a boil and add mochiko mixture a little at a time, simmering and stirring until you get the right consistency. Remove from heat and refrigerate overnight. Flavors in this stew are best if given a chance to blend.

# Hale'iwa Barbecued Pork Ribs

Cook this dish ahead of time. A quick reheat over the coals or in the oven makes the flavor twice as good. Be sure to make a big batch as eating outdoors stimulates the appetite. Look for a charcoal grill with a cover and large grilling surface and, if possible, an adjustable grate and firebox. To light a charcoal grill, skip the lighter fluid, which can give food a strange chemical aftertaste. Instead use a chimney—a cylindrical, metal apparatus that holds briquettes in a tight pile so they heat quickly. After heating the coals, pour them into your grill and get cooking. Feel the heat. Light coals about 30 minutes in advance of cooking time. To determine if the coals are ready, hold your palm five inches over the fire. If you can hold it there for only two to three seconds, the fire is hot; four or five seconds, the fire is medium; a full six seconds means that the fire is low.

Serves 4-6

**2 whole slabs pork ribs, cut into sections**
**  of 3 ribs each**
**Water to cover ribs in stockpot**
**1/2 cup sea salt**
**4 cloves garlic, whole**
**1 finger fresh ginger, whole**
**2 green onion, whole**

**Hale'iwa Barbecue Sauce:**

**1 teaspoon red chili flakes**
**2 (15-ounce) cans tomato sauce**
**2 cups brown sugar**
**1/2 cup vinegar**
**1/2 cup honey**
**2 cups onion, minced**
**2 teaspoons liquid smoke**
**2 teaspoons chili powder**
**1 teaspoon coarsely cracked black pepper**
**2 tablespoons steak sauce**
**1/2 teaspoon dry mustard**
**1 cinnamon stick**
**1 cup canned crushed pineapple**
**1 tablespoon fresh garlic, minced**

Combine all Hale'iwa Barbecue Sauce ingredients in a saucepan, bring to a boil, reduce heat, and simmer 1 hour. Strain and set aside.

Place ribs in stockpot and cover with water. Start with 1/2 cup sea salt and keep adding until water tastes salty, then add garlic, ginger, and green onions. Bring to a boil. Reduce heat and let simmer 45 to 60 minutes, or until ribs are tender. Remove ribs from stockpot and let cool.

Heat a hibachi until coals are hot. Brush ribs with barbecue sauce and grill until thoroughly heated. Baste the ribs with barbecue sauce as they cook.

# Honomalino Lamb with Satay Sauce

This lamb (Colorado-raised lamb is also recommended) raised on grasses and macadamia leaves in the western part of the Big Island receives Asian embellishments of a spicy marinade and a coconut-laced peanut sauce. Satay, a peanut sauce, is popular in Thailand and Southeast Asia and is a complement to grilled meats and tofu. Red curry paste increases the complexity of the sauce.

Serves 8

2 to 2-1/2 pounds boneless lamb loin

**Marinade:**

2 tablespoons soy sauce

2 tablespoons sugar

2 tablespoons hoisin sauce (sweet-spicy soybean-garlic sauce)

2 tablespoons canola oil

1 tablespoon garlic, minced

1 tablespoon fresh ginger, minced

1 tablespoon cilantro

1 tablespoon fresh basil, minced

1/2 teaspoon red chili pepper flakes

Salt and pepper to taste

**Satay Sauce:**

2 tablespoons canola oil

1/2 cup onion, minced

1 teaspoon ginger, minced

1 teaspoon garlic, minced

1 cup fresh Thai basil, minced

3/4 cup peanut butter

2 tablespoons orange juice

2 teaspoons sugar

1/2 teaspoon chili-garlic sauce (or 1/4 teaspoon red chili pepper flakes)

1-1/2 cups coconut milk

To marinate the meat:

Combine marinade ingredients and rub mixture into lamb. Marinate 4 to 6 hours in refrigerator, turning lamb occasionally. Broil lamb to desired doneness. Slice and serve with Satay Sauce.

To prepare the Satay Sauce:

Heat oil in a saucepan and sauté onion, ginger, garlic, and basil until onion is translucent. Stir in peanut butter, orange juice, sugar, and chili garlic sauce. Cook on low heat 15 minutes, stirring occasionally. Stir in coconut milk and cook until heated through. Cool to room temperature.

# Ka'ū Mac Nut-Crusted Roast Loin of Pork with Tropical Marmalade

Crown a pork roast with rich macadamias and a refreshing medley of island fruits. Pohā, the cape gooseberry and a member of the Rose family, adds a distinctive tart taste to the medley. The calyxes of the green pōha flowers swell into pale green berries. As the berries ripen, they turn yellow-green or even orange.

Serves 8

1 boneless pork loin (3 pounds)

1 tablespoon soy sauce

1 tablespoon garlic, minced

1/2 teaspoon salt

1/2 teaspoon cracked black pepper

1-1/2 cups Portuguese (or Easter) sweet breadcrumbs

3/4 cup finely chopped macadamia nuts

1/2 cup pohā (cape gooseberry) jelly (available in Island markets and kitchen-specialty shops)

1/2 cup butter, softened

1 tablespoon parsley, minced

2 teaspoons paprika

**Tropical Marmalade:**

2 cups fresh pineapple, diced

3 cups fresh papaya, diced

1/2 cup fresh pohā berries

6 tablespoons sugar or to taste

Fresh mint or spearmint, chopped

1/8 teaspoon prepared horseradish or to taste, optional

To prepare the Tropical Marmalade:

In a saucepan combine all ingredients except mint or spearmint. Bring to a boil, then simmer, stirring every 5 minutes to avoid scorching, for 1 hour or until mixture reaches jam consistency. Cool. Then fold in the fresh mint or spearmint to taste.

To roast the pork:

Preheat oven to 350 degrees. Season loin with soy sauce, garlic, salt, and black pepper; let stand 20 minutes. Roast for 45 minutes.

Meanwhile, combine breadcrumbs, macadamia nuts, pohā jelly, butter, parsley, and paprika; mix well. Ten minutes before the end of cooking time, remove roast from oven and coat loin with crumb mixture. Return loin to oven and roast 10 minutes.

Let stand 10 minutes before carving.

Serve with Tropical Marmalade.

# Paniolo Steak

This recipe originated with the Hawaiian cowboys (paniolo). Brush the meats you are grilling with sauces only during the last 20 minutes of cooking to prevent over-browning or burning. Avoid over-grilling.

Serves 4

4 (10-ounce) New York steaks

**Basic Teriyaki Sauce (makes 4-1/2 cups):**
2 cups soy sauce
1 cup mirin
1 cup water
1/2 cup brown sugar, packed
3 teaspoons garlic, minced
3 teaspoons ginger, minced

**Steaks:**
1 tablespoon cornstarch
1 tablespoon water

**Garnish:**
Pineapple wedges
Toasted coconut flakes

To prepare the Basic Teriyaki Sauce:

Combine soy sauce, mirin, water, brown sugar, garlic, and ginger. Whisk to blend. Reserve one cup and set aside.

Pour remaining sauce over steaks. Marinate 4 to 6 hours, turning occasionally.

Blend cornstarch and water to make smooth paste; bring reserved teriyaki sauce to a boil. Stir in cornstarch mixture to make a glaze. Reduce heat and simmer, stirring frequently and set aside.

Broil or grill steaks, basting with teriyaki glaze, until cooked to desired doneness.

Broil pineapple wedges and sprinkle with toasted coconut.

Rae Huo

# Papa Choy's Beef Tomato

Watching my father chop vegetables at the speed of light, then stir-fry them with paper-thin slices of beef, was a treat to the eyes as well as the taste buds. Even the marinade and the sauce take only minutes to mix. Make sure the rice is ready.

Serves 6

1 pound round or flank steak
1 tablespoon oil
3 medium fresh tomatoes, cut into wedges
1 medium onion, sliced into half moons
1 large green pepper, sliced into strips
4 stalks green onion, cut into 1-inch lengths
2 stalks celery, thinly sliced diagonally
Salt and pepper to taste

**Papa Choy's Beef Marinade (Makes 1/4 cup):**
1 tablespoon soy sauce
1 tablespoon sherry
1 tablespoon oil
1-1/2 teaspoons granulated sugar
1 clove garlic, minced
1/4 finger fresh ginger, sliced

**Papa Choy's Sauce (Makes 1-1/4 cups):**
1 cup chicken broth
1 tablespoon cornstarch
2 tablespoons soy sauce
2 teaspoons salt
2 teaspoons brown sugar
1 teaspoon oyster sauce

To prepare the Beef Marinade:
Mix all ingredients together and set aside.

To prepare the sauce:
Combine all ingredients, mix well, and set aside.

Slice beef into thin strips or bite-size pieces; massage Beef Marinade into meat. Marinate for 30 minutes.

Heat 1 tablespoon oil in a wok or frying pan on medium-high. Stir-fry beef about 2 minutes and remove from pan; set aside. Add vegetables to pan and stir-fry until onions are translucent, about 3 minutes. Add Papa Choy's Sauce to vegetables and cook 2 minutes or until it comes to a boil. Add beef and adjust seasonings with salt and pepper. Serve over hot rice.

# Asian Braised Short Ribs

Braising means to sear meat, then submerge it in a small amount of liquid or fat in a covered pot, and cook it slowly until fork-tender. It is a classic technique for less tender cuts of meat.

**Serves 4**

**4 short ribs, about 2-inches thick**
**Salt and pepper to taste**
**1/2 cup flour for dusting meat**
**3 tablespoons oil**
**4 cloves garlic, crushed**
**1/4 cup carrots, coarsely chopped**
**1/2 cup onions, coarsely chopped**
**3 tablespoons cilantro**
**3/4 cup soy sauce**
**Enough chicken broth or stock to cover meat**
**1-1/2 cup sugar**
**1/2 cup sherry**

Sprinkle short ribs with salt and pepper, dust with flour, then brown in 3 tablespoons oil in large braising pan for 1 or 2 minutes per side.

Add garlic, carrots, onion, cilantro, and soy sauce. Brown it all together for another 5 minutes. Cover with chicken broth or stock.

Bring to a boil and add sugar and sherry.

Cover with foil or ovenproof lid and braise at 350 degrees for 1 to 2 hours or until fork-tender.

# fish & seafood

# Broiled Lobster with Basil-Garlic Butter Sauce and Grilled Corn Relish

Lobsters barbecue well because they come in their own self-contained package. Just throw them over the coals, cover the grill, and let them cook, or broil them in the oven. The meat stays quite moist, protected by the hard shell. Lobster is traditionally served with butter; adding a little basil to the butter is the perfect touch to spice up the flavor. Look for garlic heads with small cloves because they are sweeter. The larger cloves have a bitter sprout inside which should be removed.

## Serves 1-2

1-1/2 pounds fresh, live Maine lobster
Salt and pepper to taste
Basil-Garlic Butter Sauce (see recipe)
Grilled Corn Relish (see recipe below)

**Garnish:**
Lemon wedges

**Basil-Garlic Butter Sauce:**
6 tablespoons butter, softened
2 teaspoons fresh garlic, puréed
1 tablespoon fresh basil, minced
Juice of 1/2 fresh lemon
Salt and pepper to taste

**Grilled Corn Relish:**
1/2 onion, chopped
1/2 cup red pepper, chopped
2 tablespoons light olive oil
1 teaspoon garlic, minced
3 corn cobs, grilled then shucked
Salt and pepper to taste
1/4 cup cilantro, coarsely chopped

To prepare the Basil-Garlic Butter Sauce:
Heat butter, and add the rest of the ingredients, except basil. Cook until garlic is translucent. Add basil and cook for 30 seconds.

To prepare the Grilled Corn Relish:
Sauté onions and pepper with olive oil. Add garlic and grilled corn kernels. Add salt and pepper to taste. Fold in cilantro.

Cut lobster in half, season with salt and pepper, and broil until cooked.

To serve, place lobster on a platter, and drizzle with Basil-Garlic Butter Sauce, or serve Basil-Garlic Butter Sauce in ramekin dish on the side for dipping. Garnish lobster with lemon wedges, and serve with Grilled Corn Relish.

# Chef Sam's Wok-Seared Scallops

The hardest thing about wok-seared scallops is the preparation. Once you put the scallops in the wok, in two minutes your guests will be saying, "Wow." Ginger, garlic, and scallops are a perfect marriage of flavors. The pure taste of the scallop is one important thing. Not overcooking is even more important. Think delicate!

**Serves 4**

3/4 pound fresh scallops (see note)
2 teaspoons cornstarch
1/2 teaspoon salt

**Sauce:**
1/4 cup tomato sauce
1/4 cup rice wine or dry sherry
2 teaspoons chili garlic sauce (sambal)
2 teaspoons oyster sauce
1-1/2 teaspoons granulated sugar

2 tablespoons oil, divided use
1 teaspoon minced fresh garlic
1 teaspoon peeled and minced ginger

Pat scallops dry with paper towels and sprinkle with salt. Place in a small bowl with cornstarch and salt. Let stand for 5 minutes.

Meanwhile, combine tomato sauce, rice wine, chili garlic sauce, oyster sauce, and sugar and mix until sugar is dissolved. Set aside.

Coat wok with 1 tablespoon of oil and heat over high heat. Add garlic and ginger and cook for about 10 seconds, stirring constantly. Add tomato sauce mixture and simmer over medium heat for 2 to 3 minutes. Remove from heat and keep warm.

In a second wok (you can also use a skillet or frying pan), add remaining oil and heat over medium-high until hot. Add 1 tablespoon of oil, coating the sides. Add scallops and cook until they turn opaque in color. This takes about 2 minutes on each side. Pour sauce on a serving plate and arrange scallops on the sauce.

Wonderful as is or better when served with your favorite vegetable.

**Note:** Scallops are quite perishable. Fresh scallops should have a sweet, mild odor and feel slightly springy. Once purchased, refrigerate them in a plastic bag over a bowl of ice.

# Coconut Mac-Nut Shrimp
## with Guava Sweet & Sour Sauce

This dish blends a variety of textures, flavors, and aromas. Adding the coconut flakes makes all the difference. The shrimps will crisp up into spiny-looking prongs that crackle when you bite into them. Panko is a Japanese-style breadcrumb mixture that gives an extra crunchy texture to foods.

Serves 4

**24 pieces shrimp (21/25 count), cleaned and shelled**

**1 cup all-purpose flour**

**1 cup coconut flakes**

**1 cup roasted macadamia nuts, crushed**

**2-1/2 cups panko (Japanese style crispy breadcrumbs)**

**3 or 4 whole eggs, whipped**

**4 cups vegetable oil**

**Salt and pepper to taste**

**Sam Choy's Guava Sweet & Sour Sauce:**
**1/2 cup ketchup**
**1/2 cup white wine vinegar**
**1/2 cup water**
**2 teaspoons soy sauce**
**1/2 cup granulated sugar**
**1/4 cup frozen guava concentrate, undiluted**
**1-1/2 teaspoons fresh garlic, minced**
**1/4 teaspoon hot pepper sauce**
**1/4 cup pineapple juice**
**4 tablespoons cornstarch mixed with 3 tablespoons water, for thickening**

### To prepare shrimp:

Mix coconut flakes, macadamia nuts, and panko together. Dredge the shrimp in flour, egg, and then in coconut flake-macadamia nut-panko mixture. Season with salt and pepper. Deep-fry until golden brown.

Serve with Sam Choy's Guava Sweet & Sour Sauce.

### Sam Choy's Guava Sweet & Source Sauce:

In a medium saucepan, combine all sweet and sour ingredients except cornstarch mixture. Blend well, bring to a boil, then add cornstarch mixture. Reduce heat and simmer, stirring frequently until thickened.

# Crusted Ono as Featured at Sam Choy's Restaurants

Crusted ono is one of the most popular dishes in our restaurants. People love it. It's very, very good. When you combine macadamia nuts and panko, it keeps the ono moist on the inside and crispy on the outside. Marlin, 'ahi, or mahi mahi (dolphin fish) can be substituted.

Serves 4

4 (6-ounce) ono (wahoo) fillets
1/4 cup olive oil
1 teaspoon fresh ginger, minced
1 teaspoon garlic, minced
Salt and pepper to taste
1/2 cup cracker crumbs
1/2 cup butter at room temperature
1/4 cup macadamia nuts, chopped
1 tablespoon fresh herbs, minced
   (combination of basil, dill, and thyme)
1 teaspoon paprika

**Papaya-Mango Salsa: (Makes 2-1/2 cups)**
3 tablespoons sugar
1-1/2 tablespoons vinegar
Pinch red chili pepper flakes
Pinch cumin
1 medium papaya, seeded, peeled, and diced
1 cup mango, peeled and diced
1/2 small red onion, diced
3 tablespoons red bell pepper, diced
2 tablespoons cilantro, chopped

**To prepare the Papaya-Mango Salsa:**
Mix sugar, vinegar, chili flakes, and cumin until sugar dissolves. Fold in remaining ingredients. Set salsa aside.

**To prepare the fish:**
Marinate ono in mixture of olive oil, ginger, garlic, salt, and pepper.

Preheat oven to 375 degrees. Combine cracker crumbs, butter, macadamia nuts, herbs, and paprika; blend well. Divide cracker-crumb mixture into 4 portions and pat 1 portion on top of each fillet. Bake 8 to 10 minutes.

Serve with Papaya-Mango Salsa.

**Note:** If ono cannot be obtained, substitute an equal portion of any firm white-fleshed fish.

# Furikake-Kakimochi Crusted 'Ahi Steaks on a Bed of Crispy Dried Shrimp and Green Beans

Furikake is a mixture of dried seaweed, fish flakes, and other seasonings used on some Japanese foods. Kakimochi are wonderful sweet-salty Japanese rice crackers, and a favorite snack food in Hawai'i. When the crackers are crumbled and mixed with furikake, the result is a tangy, tasty breading mixture that takes an already delicious 'ahi steak from great to sublime.

Serves 1-2 (multiply to increase serving)

**Furikake and Kakimochi Mixture (see note)**
**6-ounce 'ahi steak (yellowfin tuna)**
**Wasabi paste**
**1 teaspoon canola oil**
**3 tablespoons dried shrimp**
**1 package (10 ounces) frozen French-cut green beans, thawed**
**1 teaspoon chili garlic paste**
**1 teaspoon hondashi**

Crush Furikake and Kakimochi Mixture until crumb-like. Set aside.

Smear 'ahi steak with wasabi paste on one side and dip into Furikake-Kakimochi Mixture.

Coat wok with oil and heat until hot. Sear 'ahi until medium rare. Remove from wok. Add dried shrimp to wok and stir until golden brown in color. Add green beans and stir for 30 seconds then add chili paste and sprinkle in hondashi. Stir-fry for another minute and serve hot. Enjoy!

## Note:
Furikake and kakimochi are found in every Hawai'i supermarket. If mainland supermarkets don't carry them, try an Asian market. Mix to suit your taste. Some cooks like lots of furikake, some like less.

# Ginger Pesto-Crusted 'Ōpakapaka
## with Coconut Cream Sauce

If the Coconut Cream Sauce isn't thick enough, don't panic. Just add enough cornstarch mixture to thicken the simmering sauce as desired, and cook for another minute. Adjust the seasoning with salt and pepper.

Serves 4

8 (3-ounces each) fresh 'ōpakapaka (pink
  snapper) fillets
1 tablespoon oil, for frying
Ginger Pesto Sauce (see recipe below)
Coconut Cream Sauce (see recipe below)

**Garnish:**
**Tomato wedges**
**Enoki mushrooms (straw)**

**Ginger Pesto Sauce:**
1/2 cup fresh cilantro, minced
1/2 cup green onion, minced
1/4 cup fresh ginger, minced
3/4 cup peanut oil
1 tablespoon soy sauce
Salt and white pepper to taste

**Coconut Cream Sauce:**
3 tablespoons butter
1 medium round onion, minced
1 cup heavy cream
2 cups canned coconut milk (unsweetened)
2 tablespoons cornstarch mixed with 1-1/2
  tablespoons water, if needed for thickening
Salt and pepper to taste

To prepare the Ginger Pesto Sauce:
Place cilantro, green onions, and ginger in a deep bowl. Heat peanut oil in a pan until smoking. Pour heated oil over cilantro, green onions, and ginger. BE CAREFUL: THE OIL WILL BE SIZZLING AND VERY HOT. Add soy sauce and salt and pepper to taste. Set aside.

To prepare the Coconut Cream Sauce:
Place butter in a saucepan. Add onions and cook until translucent. Add heavy cream. Bring to a boil, reduce heat and simmer for 1 to 2 minutes. Add coconut milk and cook for another 2 minutes. Set aside.

To prepare the 'ōpakapaka:
Marinate 'ōpakapaka in cooled Ginger Pesto Sauce for 1 to 2 minutes. Place fillet in a frying pan, and cook for 1-1/2 to 2 minutes on each side over medium-high heat.

Pour 2 ounces of Coconut Cream Sauce on each of 4 serving plates. Arrange two pieces of fish on each plate, and drizzle with Ginger Pesto Sauce.

Rae Huo

# Gingered Crab

Ginger root is a small brown plant which takes its name from an old Sanskrit word that means "horn-root," referring to its knobby shape. Its skin is similar to that of a potato, but once peeled, the insides are anything but bland. It's a very popular spice in Asian cuisine. The most efficient and economical way to scrape off the brown skin is with a spoon.

Serves 3-4

**3-pound Dungeness crab**
**3 tablespoons oil**
**1/2 cup julienne ginger**
**2 cups chicken stock**
**1-1/2 tablespoons cornstarch**
**2 tablespoons water**
**4 green onion, cut into julienne strips**

**To prepare the crab:**

Clean crab. Remove the top shell and separate the claws from the body. Crack the claws into serving-size pieces. Leave the body intact.

Heat oil in wok and stir-fry crab and 1/4 cup of the ginger for 1 minute. Add 1 cup of the chicken stock; cover and steam for 5 minutes.

Remove crab to a heated serving platter.

Add the remaining cup of chicken stock and bring to a boil. Blend cornstarch and water to make a smooth paste. Stir cornstarch mixture into chicken stock. Reduce heat and simmer, stirring frequently, until thickened. Stir in the remaining 1/4 cup ginger and green onions. Pour over crab and serve immediately.

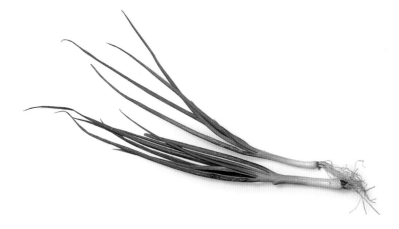

# Gingered Scallops with Colorful Soba Noodles

This soba salad is enlivened by the tastes and colors of the carrot, zucchini, red bell pepper, and scallops. It's a variation of the traditional local somen salad.

## Serves 6

1-1/2 pounds scallops

2 teaspoons canola oil

1/2 pound soba (Japanese thin brown buckwheat noodles)

**Marinade:**

1-1/2 tablespoons dry white wine

1-1/2 tablespoons orange juice

1 tablespoon ginger, minced

1 tablespoon red bell pepper, minced (or 1 Hawaiian red chili pepper, seeded and minced)

1 tablespoon yellow bell pepper, minced

1 tablespoon fresh basil, chopped

1 tablespoon cilantro, minced

1/2 teaspoon sugar

Salt and white pepper to taste

In a bowl, combine marinade ingredients and marinate scallops.

Cook soba according to package directions; drain.

In a large mixing bowl, combine soba with Pasta Mixture ingredients. Toss as you would salad greens.

## Pasta Mixture:

| | |
|---|---|
| 12 fresh spinach leaves | 1 tablespoon cilantro, minced |
| 1/2 cup julienne carrots | 1 tablespoon soy sauce |
| 1/2 cup julienne red bell pepper | 1 tablespoon olive oil |
| 1/2 cup julienne zucchini | 1 teaspoon sesame seed oil |
| 12 fresh basil leaves | 1 teaspoon garlic, minced |

In a skillet, heat oil over medium heat and sauté scallops 1-1/2 minutes on each side; do not overcook. Pour scallops and juices right over soba.

# Hilo Mango-Liliko'i-Basil Barbecue Shrimp

Mango has a flavor of its own. Liliko'i (passion fruit) blends with all the spicy marinated shrimp-on-a-skewer. Sprinkle basil on top. Mangoes are indigenous to southern Asia; they were brought to Hawai'i from Manila in 1824. They are good to excellent sources of pro-Vitamin A. The different varieties of mangoes vary greatly in Vitamin C content. (Common mangos have the most Vitamin C.)

Serves 4

1 pound shrimp (16/20 count)
2 large mangoes, each cut in 6 large chunks

**Marinade:**
1/2 cup mango purée
1/2 cup frozen liliko'i concentrate, thawed
1 tablespoon brown sugar
1 tablespoon fresh basil, minced
1 tablespoon fresh dill, chopped
1 teaspoon fresh ginger, minced
1/2 teaspoon garlic, minced

Peel and devein shrimp, leaving tails on. Combine marinade ingredients and marinate shrimp for 1 hour.

On each of four skewers, alternately thread shrimp and mango chunks.

Grill or broil kabobs for 7 minutes, or until shrimp is cooked, turning once and basting occasionally with marinade.

# Speared Kahuku Prawns

These guys don't lose their heads (or tails)! Take the time to spear the prawn with the carrot and broccoli. They cook so quickly and are eye-appealing resting on the mushroom cap. This is a real dress-up dish.

## Serves 5

2 pounds large prawns (10 per pound)

1/2 pound broccoli florets with stalk attached

1 carrot, cut into 20 strips about 2-1/2 inches in length

1 cup chicken stock or low-sodium chicken broth

1 tablespoon soy sauce

1 tablespoon sherry

1 teaspoon ginger, peeled and minced

1 teaspoon fresh garlic, minced

1 tablespoon cornstarch

2 tablespoons canola oil

20 fresh shiitake mushrooms, rinsed

**To prepare the prawns:**

Peel shell from tail of prawns, leaving head and tail attached; devein. Make two slits in the back of each prawn for spearing with broccoli and carrots. Spear each prawn with a broccoli floret stalk and a carrot strip.

Combine chicken stock, soy sauce, sherry, ginger, garlic, and cornstarch; blend well.

Heat canola oil in a wok and gently stir-fry prawns, about 2 minutes. Remove prawns from wok.

Add stock mixture to wok and bring to a boil. Reduce heat and simmer, stirring frequently, until thickened. Add prawns and shiitake mushrooms; cook 1 minute.

To serve, place each prawn on top of a destemmed mushroom cap.

# Miso Yaki Salmon

Miso, a favorite seasoning in Japan, is made from fermented soybeans mixed with crushed grain. There are two types commonly available in grocery stores—white miso made with rice and red miso made with barley. They also come in plastic tubes found in the refrigerated foods sections. The white miso, 'shiromiso,' is somewhat sweet in flavor. It is a good all-purpose soybean paste for flavoring soups or creating salad dressings. 'Akamiso' is reddish brown and salty, robust in flavor and is usually used to marinate meats, especially when grilled.

Serves 4

4 (6-ounce) salmon fillets

**Miso Marinade:**
3/4 cup white miso
3 tablespoons fresh ginger, grated
1/4 cup granulated sugar
1/2 cup mirin (Japanese sweet rice wine)
1/4 cup rice vinegar

**Garnish:**
Roasted sesame seeds
Lemon wedges

To prepare the Miso Marinade:
Blend all ingredients. Marinate salmon fillets in Miso Marinade for 1 hour.

Broil salmon fillets for 8 to 10 minutes.

Serve with hot rice, and garnish with roasted sesame seeds and lemon wedges.

# Ono Kiev with Mango Coulis

When I was growing up, I always loved the traditional chicken kiev. Since I live in Hawai'i where fish is abundant, I put a twist on it using seafood. Freeze any over-supply of mangoes, peeled and cut, core removed, for later use in preserves, pies or breads, but be sure to use within six months. You can substitute striped marlin, 'ahi, or mahi mahi (dolphin fish) for the ono.

Serves 4

4 (6-ounce) ono fillets
Flour for dusting
2 egg whites, lightly beaten
3/4 cup macadamia nuts, finely chopped
2 tablespoons oil

**Herbal Butter:**
1/4 cup butter, softened
1 tablespoon cilantro, minced
1 teaspoon fresh lemon juice
Salt and coarsely ground black pepper to
   taste

**Mango Coulis:**
1 ripe mango, peeled and cubed
1 tablespoon white vinegar
1 tablespoon sugar
1/4 cup cilantro, finely chopped

Preheat oven to 350 degrees.

To prepare the Herbal Butter:
Blend together all ingredients. Shape mixture into a log 1/2-inch in diameter and freeze until firm. Cut into four sections. Set aside.

To prepare the Mango Coulis:
Dice 1/2 cup of the mango. Purée the remaining mango in a food processor or blender. In a small saucepan combine mango purée, white vinegar, and sugar; cook for 5 minutes. Stir in cilantro. Set aside.

To prepare the fish:
Roll each fillet around one Herbal Butter log. Coat ono fillets with flour; dip in egg whites, and coat with macadamia nuts. In a skillet heat oil and sauté fish until lightly browned. Place fillets on a baking sheet and bake for 7 to 8 minutes.

Spoon Mango Coulis onto individual plates and top with fillet.

Rae Huo

# Sam Choy's Garlic Ginger Salmon

The trick with salmon is to stop cooking it before it looks done. The fish keeps cooking even after you remove it from the heat. To select fresh ginger, look for a root that is firm, without soft spots, and has "thumbs" that can be easily broken off. To use ginger root, cut off the amount you need and peel it with the edge of a spoon. To store, scrub the skin with water and wrap the ginger well before putting it in the refrigerator. If well-wrapped, it will keep for several weeks.

Serves 4

**4 (6-ounce) salmon fillets**

**Poaching Water:**

**4 cups water**

**1/2 cup chopped cilantro**

**2 cups white wine**

**1/3 cup peeled and diced carrots**

**1/3 cup diced onions**

**1/3 cup diced celery**

**Juice of 1 lemon**

**1 teaspoon salt**

**1/2 teaspoon cracked black pepper**

**Bottled Sam Choy's Garlic Ginger Sauce**

Cut each salmon fillet into two pieces. Set aside.

In a wok, mix Poaching Water ingredients and bring to a boil. Poach salmon about 3 to 4 minutes, depending on thickness of fillets. As soon as salmon turns opaque, remove from wok. Be careful not to overcook salmon.

To serve, generously drizzle Sam Choy's Garlic Ginger Sauce on plate. Top with salmon fillets and again drizzle top of fish with Sam Choy's Garlic Ginger Sauce. Serve with your favorite vegetable and your favorite rice.

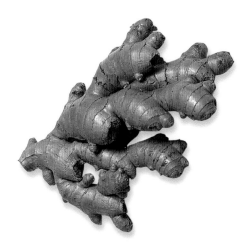

# Steamed 'Ōpakapaka with Shiitake Mushrooms and Butter Soy Sauce

The 'ōpakapaka, red snapper, has a firm texture when teamed with the subtle smoky flavor of this "Japanese black mushroom." A traditional French butter sauce is given an oriental twist with a dash of soy sauce and a sprinkling of cilantro. Dried shiitake have a more concentrated flavor than fresh shiitake. If using dried mushrooms, soak them to re-hydrate and soften them before using.

### Serves 4

**4 (6-ounce) 'ōpakapaka fillets**
**1/4 cup oil**
**3 tablespoons soy sauce**
**1 teaspoon ginger, minced**
**2 tablespoons butter**
**2 cups sliced fresh shiitake mushrooms**
**1/4 cup cilantro, chopped**
**Salt and pepper to taste**

Marinate 'ōpakapaka fillets for 1 hour in a combination of oil, 2 tablespoons of the soy sauce, and ginger.

Steam fillets 8 to 10 minutes or until fish flakes easily when tested with a fork. Set aside on a heated platter.

In a heavy skillet, melt butter; add shiitake mushrooms and sauté until just limp. Add the remaining 1 tablespoon soy sauce and cilantro. Season to taste with salt and pepper. Pour shiitake mushroom mixture over fillets.

Rae Huo

# Cold Tahitian Lobster

Lobster always excites people. This particular cold presentation is as dramatic as it is delicious and can be prepared ahead of time and held in the fridge. It looks like it took a long time and a lot of trouble, but it's really simple.

## Serves 1 to 2

1 (1-1/2 pound) lobster

Juice of 1 lemon

1 teaspoon cracked peppercorns

2 bay leaves

1 clove garlic, crushed

1 beer

2 tablespoon asparagus, chopped (parboil until tender before chopping)

2 tablespoons green peas

2 tablespoons carrots, diced (parboiled 2–3 minutes)

1/2 teaspoons Chinese parsley, minced

1/2 teaspoon fresh dill

1/2 cup fresh spinach, chopped (or frozen cooked spinach, squeezed)

2 tablespoons water chestnuts, diced

Salt and pepper to taste

1 cup mayonnaise, or to taste

1/2 teaspoon curry powder, or to taste

**Garnish:**

Lemon wedges

Fresh dill sprig

### To prepare the lobster:

Steam lobster for 6 to 8 minutes over boiling water to which you have added lemon juice, cracked peppercorns, bay leaves, garlic, and beer. Remove lobster from steamer when cooked and immediately submerge in ice water. Let remain in ice water until chilled, about 15 to 20 minutes.

### To prepare the salad:

While lobster cools, make the salad by mixing all remaining ingredients except for the mayonnaise and curry powder. Blend mayonnaise and curry powder together then mix thoroughly with vegetables.

Split the lobster in two, remove tail meat, discard innards, and reserve shell. Fill shell about half full with salad mix, reserving about 1/2 cup of the mix. Slice tail meat into 3 or 4 sections and replace in tail over salad, leaving gaps between sections to be filled with reserved salad mix. Crack claws and use for garnish.

Arrange stuffed lobster and cracked claws on bed of finely chopped lettuce and garnish with lemon wedges and a sprig of fresh dill.

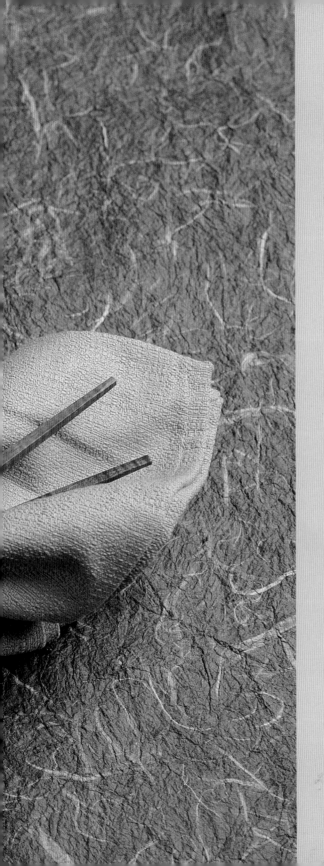

# sides & vegetables

# Baked Coconut Taro

Taro has been a staple in Hawai'i from earliest times to the present. The entire plant is eaten, from its starchy root (often mashed into poi) to its heart-shaped leaves (known as lū'au). Over 300 varieties of taro are cultivated world-wide; 86 of those varieties are grown in Hawai'i. Wetland taro is grown in flooded valley fields and is best for poi. Dryland or upland taro tolerates dryer conditions and can be cultivated in the uplands. In this recipe, the sweetness of the coconut syrup mix enhances the flavor of the taro.

Serves 4

1 pound fresh taro root, blanched and cubed
1/4 cup butter
1/4 cup coconut syrup
Salt and pepper to taste

**Garnish:**
1/4 c up coconut flakes, toasted on skillet or
    under broiler
Macadamia nuts, roasted and chopped

Combine all ingredients in a covered casserole dish and bake at 350 degrees for 35 minutes.

To serve, garnish with coconut flakes and macadamia nuts.

# Garlic Mashed Potatoes

Garlic mashed potatoes are a favorite accompaniment to chicken main courses. Russet potatoes give the fluffiest texture. Raw garlic is usually pungent and slightly bitter, but when cooked with the potatoes it becomes mild and sweet.

Serves 4–6

**Makes about 6 cups**

**2-1/4 pounds potatoes**
**4 whole cloves garlic**
**1/2 pound butter**
**6 tablespoons heavy cream**
**Salt and white pepper to taste**

Fill a large pot with three inches of cold water. Add the potatoes. You can add them as whole potatoes, and remove the skins later, or peel them and cut them into 1-inch cubes. Add enough cold water to cover the potatoes, then the cloves of garlic, and bring to a boil. Cook for 8 to 10 minutes, or until the potatoes are tender. Drain.

If you have boiled the potatoes whole, remove the skins. Purée the potatoes and garlic. You can use a food processor, an electric mixer, a ricer, a food mill, or—if you don't mind the lumps—a potato masher. Add the butter and cream and mix well. Season with salt and white pepper. Serve immediately.

# Pan-Fried Spicy Eggplant

Eggplant and chili paste team up in the wok for an easy, popular favorite packed with flavor. Great with a bowl of rice.

Serves 4

3 tablespoons olive oil

2 cloves garlic, minced

2 medium Asian eggplants, peeled and cut in 1-inch sections

2 tablespoons soy sauce

1-1/2 tablespoons brown sugar

1 tablespoon garlic-chili sauce, available in Asian section of markets

1 cup chicken stock

1/8 teaspoon white pepper

In a wok, heat oil and add garlic, eggplant, soy sauce, sugar, and chili sauce. Sauté 2 or 3 minutes. Add chicken stock and white pepper. Cover and simmer 8 to 10 minutes. Serve over rice.

# Sam Choy's Island Lup Cheong Fried Rice

If you always wondered what to do with leftover rice, here is the answer. When making rice, make sure to have 3 cups leftover for this recipe. It works because rice picks up the flavor so well. This is the real traditional fried rice.

**Serves 4**

3 pieces lup cheong (Chinese pork sausage)

1 tablespoon vegetable oil

1/4 cup onion, diced

1/4 cup celery, minced

1/4 cup carrots, peeled and diced

1 teaspoon garlic, finely chopped

1 teaspoon ginger, peeled and finely chopped

1 tablespoon soy sauce

1-1/2 tablespoons oyster sauce

3 cups cooked day-old white rice

**Garnish:**

1/4 cup green onion, thinly sliced

1/4 cup red and white kamaboko (fishcake), minced

Cut lup cheong into thin diagonal slices. In a large wok, heat oil and add lup cheong. Stir-fry for about 2 minutes on medium-high heat. Add onion, celery, carrots, garlic, ginger, and stir-fry for 2 to 3 minutes over medium-high heat. Add soy and oyster sauces and then rice and toss quickly.

Serve in a large bowl garnished with green onion and kamaboko.

# Stir-Fried Mushrooms and Tofu

Stir-fry is a basic oriental style of cooking. The quick frying of the ingredients keeps the integrity of the vegetables intact, at the same time melding the flavors together. A healthy dish with eye-appeal. Made from soy beans, tofu is a great source of protein and calcium. This curd is available in many textures—silky, soft, firm, or deep fried.

Serves 4–6

**1/4 cup canola oil**
**1 pound block firm tofu, cubed**
**1/2 sweet onion, diced**
**2 teaspoons ginger, minced**
**2 teaspoons garlic, minced**
**1 teaspoon lemongrass, minced**
**1/2 red bell pepper, 1/2-inch diced**
**1/2 yellow bell pepper, 1/2-inch diced**
**8 ounces oyster mushrooms, stems removed, quartered**
**2 ounces fresh shiitake mushrooms, stems removed**
**2 tablespoons soy sauce**
**1-1/2 tablespoons oyster sauce**
**Salt and pepper to taste**
**Green onion, chopped for garnish**

Drain tofu block on paper towels in refrigerator for 1 hour.

Heat the oil in a wok and stir fry the onion, garlic, ginger, and lemongrass for 30 seconds on medium-high heat. Add peppers and mushrooms and stir-fry for another minute. Add tofu, soy sauce, and oyster sauce, and continue cooking for another minute. Season with salt to taste.

Garnish with chopped green onion.

# lū'au foods

# Assorted Seafood Laulau

Laulau is one of the main dishes featured in a Hawaiian lū'au. Meat, fish, or shellfish are layered with vegetables, tied into a bundle of ti leaves, and steamed until tender. In my version of laulau, mahi mahi, scallops, and shrimp all become close friends. A soy sauce-mayonnaise mixture forms a rich moist layer between the seafood and the vegetables. Steam to perfection and serve to delighted diners.

**Serves 2-3 (multiply to increase serving)**

6 tablespoons mayonnaise

2 teaspoons soy sauce

1 teaspoon chopped dill

Salt and pepper to taste

2 ti leaves

3 (2-1/2-ounce) pieces of fresh fish (mahi mahi or salmon is best)

1/2 cup fresh spinach leaves

1/2 cup julienne carrots

1/2 julienne zucchini

2 fresh shiitake mushrooms, rinsed and sliced

4 bay scallops, rinsed and shelled

4 bay shrimp, peeled and deveined

Other assorted seafood, optional

1 quart water

In a small bowl, combine mayonnaise, soy sauce, fresh dill, salt, and pepper. Mix well. Set aside.

**To prepare the ti leaves:**
Take 2 medium-size ti leaves and with a sharp knife remove the ribs. Then with tip of knife, barely tap the rib midway. Pull the rib completely off of the two ti leaves. On one of the leaves, split the stem to the bottom of the leaf.

**Making the laulau:**
Criss-cross the 2 ti leaves to make the base of the laulau. Add a slice of fish, then a dollop of soy sauce-mayonnaise mixture, and follow with zucchini, carrots, spinach, and a couple of slices of shiitake mushroom. Repeat this process 2 more times, stacking the fish and vegetables carefully. At the very top, add the bay shrimp, the scallops, and any fresh seafood you desire. Pull the ti-leaf stems up; wrap the split stems around the other two stems and tie them in a knot, forming a leaf pouch or bag. (Take a look at the picture to see how it's done.)

Place a steaming rack in a 4-quart pot along with 1/2 to 1-quart of water. Heat until water is at a rapid boil. Carefully place laulau in pot and cover. Steam for approximately 15 to 20 minutes, or until done.

Carefully remove laulau and serve with rice or poi.

# Chicken Long Rice

This chicken and vegetable dish is a staple in Hawaiian buffets. The transparent "bean thread" noodles in the dish may look strange to malihini (newcomers to Hawai'i) but once they savor chicken long rice, they will never pass it by again. Served with poi, green onions, and Hawaiian salt, this dish is a star of local-kine food.

Serves 6

1 (12-ounce) package long rice
3 tablespoons vegetable oil
6 pieces chicken thighs, boneless and skinless, cut into 3/4-inch cubes or chunks
3 tablespoons fresh ginger, peeled, julienne
6 cups chicken stock or chicken broth
Salt and pepper to taste
1 cup green onion, cut into 1-inch long strips, on the bias

Cover the long rice with warm water for 30 to 45 minutes. Drain and cut into 3-inch long strips.

Heat the oil in a medium pot and sauté the chicken lightly. It should be seared on the outside rather than cooked through. Add ginger. Add chicken stock, cover the pot, and simmer for about 15 to 25 minutes. Add pre-soaked long rice and simmer for about 5 to 10 minutes.

If you do not plan to serve this dish immediately, reserve 1 cup of the chicken stock. Just before serving, heat the stock and mix it into the dish. Garnish with green onion.

### Variation #1
Add sliced shiitake mushrooms (if dried, pre-soak before slicing)

### Variation #2
Add sliced carrots, celery, and round onion with the ginger and green onion

# Chicken Lū'au

Lū'au leaves are the tops of the taro plant. They are a nutritious green leafy vegetable and a great substitute for spinach. All parts of the taro plant are edible.

## Serves 6

1 pound lū'au leaves, cooked
3 cups of water
1 tablespoon Hawaiian salt
1/2 teaspoon baking soda
3/4 pound boneless chicken breast halves
2 tablespoons butter
1/2 medium onion, chopped
1 cup coconut milk
1/2 teaspoon salt

## To prepare the lū'au leaves:

Rinse lū'au leaves and trim off stems and thick veins. In a stockpot bring 3 cups of water, 1 tablespoon Hawaiian salt, and 1/2 teaspoon baking soda to a boil. Add lū'au leaves; reduce heat and cook, partially covered, for one hour. Drain and squeeze out excess liquid.

Remove skin from chicken and cut into 1-inch cubes. In a large saucepan heat butter and sauté onions until translucent. Stir in chicken and cook 3 minutes, stirring frequently. Add coconut milk, cooked lū'au leaves, and salt. Simmer for 30 minutes, or until chicken is thoroughly cooked.

Rae Huo

# Haupia

Coconut milk is not the water inside the coconut. It is the liquid made by squeezing freshly grated coconut meat that has been soaked in boiling water. You can buy coconut milk canned or frozen. If you want to make your own, mix 4 cups freshly grated coconut with 2 cups boiling water, let stand 20 minutes, then strain through a double thick cheesecloth. Squeeze the cheesecloth several times to extract as much liquid as possible. Refrigerate. This rich cream or milk provides the ultimate flavor.

Serves 16

**1 can (12 ounces) coconut milk (thawed if frozen)**

**1-1/2 cups milk**

**6 tablespoons sugar**

**6 tablespoons cornstarch**

In a large saucepan combine coconut milk and milk. Blend together sugar and cornstarch and stir into coconut milk mixture. Cook over medium heat, stirring frequently until mixture thickens. Pour into an 8-inch square baking pan. Chill. When firm, cut into small squares or triangles.

Rae Huo

# Kālua Pig

Centuries before there was barbecue, there was kālua pig. A whole pig was cooked in an imu, or earth oven, for hours, then served, falling-off-the-bone tender, to appreciative Hawaiians. Most of us can't do imu, but we can come close with recipes like the following, which keeps an old Hawaiian culinary tradition alive.

Serves 12

**4-pound pork butt**
**2 tablespoons Hawaiian salt**
**2 tablespoons liquid smoke**
**1 banana leaf**
**4 to 6 large ti leaves, ribs removed**
**2 cups water**

Score pork on all sides with 1/4-inch deep slits about 1 inch apart. Rub pork with 1 tablespoon Hawaiian salt, then rub with liquid smoke. Wrap pork in the banana leaf, then wrap completely in ti leaves. Tie with string and wrap in foil.

Preheat oven to 350 degrees. Place pork in shallow roasting pan and add 2 cups water. Roast for 4 hours.

Shred pork and let stand in 1 tablespoon Hawaiian salt dissolved in 2 cups boiling water with a few drops of liquid smoke before serving.

# Lū'au Stew

My mother's legacy lives on. In Hawai'i a lū'au is the traditional way of celebrating a special occasion. It's usually a big backyard party with good food, friends, and music. Substitute spinach when lū'au leaves are not available.

Serves 6

2 pounds lū'au leaves

3 cups water

2 tablespoons Hawaiian salt

1/2 teaspoon baking soda

1 tablespoon oil

1 cup chopped onions

2 pounds stew meat or short ribs

3 cups beef stock

2 cups water

**To prepare lū'au leaves:**

Rinse lū'au leaves and trim off stems and thick veins. In a stockpot bring water, 1 tablespoon of the Hawaiian salt, and baking soda to a boil. Add lū'au leaves; reduce heat and cook, partially covered, for 1 hour. Drain and squeeze out excess liquid.

**To prepare lū'au stew:**

In a saucepan heat oil and sauté onions until translucent.

Brown stew meat. Add beef stock, water, and the remaining 1 tablespoon Hawaiian salt. Cook until meat is fork-tender. Add lū'au leaves and simmer for 30 minutes.

Rae Huo

# My Mom's Squid Lū'au

The flesh of the octopus is very flavorful and tender if not overcooked. The sweetness of the lū'au leaves and the salty flavor of the octopus balances this dish. Squid or calamari can be substituted for octopus.

Serves 12

2 pounds calamari
3 pounds lū'au leaves
3 cups water
1 tablespoon Hawaiian salt
1/2 teaspoon baking soda
6 tablespoons butter
2 medium onions, diced
3 cups coconut milk
1-1/2 teaspoons salt
1 tablespoon sugar

Clean calamari and slice in rings, then set aside.

Wash lū'au leaves and remove stems and thick veins. In a pot boil 3 cups water with the Hawaiian salt and baking soda. Add the leaves to the boiling water and reduce heat. Simmer, partially covered, for 1 hour. Drain and squeeze out liquid.

Sauté onions and calamari in butter until the onions are translucent. Add the coconut milk, cooked lū'au leaves, salt, and sugar. Simmer for 30 minutes.

# Traditional Lomilomi Salmon

It's not a lū'au without lomilomi salmon. The sweet but acidic flavor of the tomatoes, the zing of the onions, and the salty goodness of the salmon are just what's needed to balance out the meal.

**Serves 24**

**4 cups salted salmon, diced**

**12 tomatoes, diced**

**4 small red onions, diced**

**1 cup green onion, thinly sliced**

**1 to 2 Hawaiian chili peppers or
    1/4 teaspoon red pepper flakes**

Combine all ingredients and mix well. Serve well chilled.

**Note:** Different lots of salted salmon can be more or less salty, so it's a good idea to taste it before making this dish. If it's too salty, you need to soak it overnight in enough water to cover, and then rinse it twice before using.

# drinks & desserts

# Crème Brûlée

Crème Brûlée is a rich egg custard with a crisp caramelized sugar glaze. The English, the French, and the Spanish all claim to have invented it. I believe that it is the dish first documented as "burnt cream" in a 17th century English cookbook. A favorite confection at Cambridge University, it was given the more flamboyant (or elegant) French name, "Crème Brûlée." For centuries, chefs have created and passed down their versions. This is the one I developed for my restaurants.

**Serves 4**

**1/2 cup milk**
**2 cups heavy cream**
**1/2 cup brown sugar, packed**
**6 egg yolks**
**1 teaspoon vanilla extract**
**4 tablespoons superfine sugar**

Preheat oven to 350 degrees. Set up brûlée dishes on sheet pans.

**To prepare the Crème Brûlée:**
Scald milk, half of the cream, and half of the brown sugar. Beat egg yolks in a mixing bowl. Add the remaining brown sugar and the vanilla extract to the egg yolks, and beat until smooth. Add the remaining cream to the egg yolk mixture. Gradually stir the hot cream mixture into the yolk mixture. Strain the Crème Brûlée through a strainer, and skim off the foam.

Pour Crème Brûlée mixture into 4 brûlée dishes, leaving about 1/8-inch at the top (about 5 ounces per dish). Put a sheet pan in the oven, and fill it with water to make a hot water bath. Bake at 300 degrees for 35 to 50 minutes. Rotate the sheet pan to provide for even baking and to avoid overcooking the ones in the hottest parts of the oven. Bake just until the custard sets. Test to see if dessert is done by slightly tilting the brûlée dishes; if there is a bulge in the Crème Brûlée or if it is soupy in the center, it needs to cook some more.

When finished cooking, remove from the oven and the hot water bath. Let the Crème Brûlée sit at room temperature for 30 minutes. Refrigerate custard for several hours to overnight.

Just before serving, preheat the broiler until lit is very hot. Sprinkle 1 tablespoon superfine sugar over each custard. Place the custards approximately 3 inches from the broiler. Broil until the sugar is caramelized. Allow the sugar to harden for a couple of minutes, then serve.

# Key Lime Pie

The cool, tangy flavor of Key Lime Pie is very attractive during the hot months of summer. Use Key Limes from Florida. (Key Limes are a smaller, rounder lime than the common Persian Limes.) They make the difference between a good pie and a fabulous one.

Serves 8

**Crust:**
2 cups graham cracker crumbs
1/4 cup granulated sugar
2 tablespoons butter, melted

**Filling:**
14 ounces sweetened condensed milk
3 egg yolks
1/2 cup Key lime juice

**Garnish:**
Lime rind curl
Whipped cream

To prepare the crust:
Mix all crust ingredients together. Press into greased pie pan, and bake at 325 degrees for 10 minutes. Let cool.

To prepare the filling:
Combine all filling ingredients. Add filling to cooled crust, and bake at 325 degrees for 10 to 15 minutes, until filling is set in the middle. Let pie cool. Spread 1/4 cup whipped cream evenly over top of cooled pie.

Garnish with a lime rind curl in the middle of whipped cream topping.

# Macadamia Nut Cream Pie

Nothing tastes as good as a pie shell filled to the brim with macadamia nuts, baked until golden and then chilled, cut, and served with whipped cream. No matter how full you are, you can't turn this dessert down. Pecans can be substituted if macadamia nuts are unavailable.

Serves 8

**3 egg yolks**
**3 cups milk**
**3/4 cup granulated sugar**
**1/3 cup cornstarch**
**1/4 teaspoon salt**
**2 tablespoons butter**
**1-1/2 teaspoons vanilla extract**
**1 cup roasted and chopped macadamia nuts**
**1 9-inch baked pie shell**

Combine egg yolks, milk, sugar, cornstarch, salt, and butter. Bring to a boil over medium heat, stirring constantly. Boil for one minute and remove from heat. Stir in vanilla and macadamia nuts. Pour into pie shell, cover with plastic wrap, and chill.

# Lava Flow—Get It While It's Hot!

The volcano is ready to explode your taste buds with sweet flavors. Lava Flow without the rum is an option.

**Serves 1**

**2 ounces strawberry purée**
**1 ounce light rum**
**1 ounce pineapple juice**
**1 ounce sweet & sour juice**
**1 ounce coconut syrup**
**1 ounce half & half cream**
**Ice**

**Garnish:**
**1/4 slice of pineapple**
**1 orchid**

Pour strawberry purée into a 14-ounce hurricane glass. Fill blender with ice to 1/3-full, and add all other ingredients. Purée until slushy. Tilt hurricane glass to the side, and gently pour blender purée down the inside of the glass, being careful not to disturb the strawberry purée.

**Glasses used in opposite photo, from left to right: Poco Grande, Hurricane, Vino Grande, Hurricane.**

# Loco Loco Mocha Mocha

This coffee cocktail pleases the palate. Mixing coffee liqueurs with cream is as predictable as cream in your coffee, but the pineapple juice adds an island twist and an amazing flavor.

Serves 1

**Chocolate syrup**
**Ice**
**1 ounce Coco Rum**
**1 ounce Kahlua**
**1 ounce half and half**
**3 ounces pineapple juice**
**1 ounce Kahuluacino**

Squirt chocolate syrup around the inside of a 14-ounce hurricane glass. Add ice to a standard blender container until it is 1/3 full. Add the liquid ingredients (the liqueurs, half and half, and the juice) and blend until creamy. Pour the mixture into the hurricane glass, leaving ¼ inch open at the top. Cap with the whipped cream and a dash of cocoa powder. Place the cherry on the whipped cream.

**Garnish with:**

Chocolate syrup
3 tablespoons whipped cream
Cocoa powder (for dusting)

1 maraschino cherry

# Over the Rainbow

Flavors of melon, pineapple, and cranberry build a tower of refreshing taste. A fruit-filled tropical cocktail creates excitement.

Serves 1

**Ice**
**1 ounce Malibu rum**
**2 ounces pineapple juice**
**2 ounces cranberry juice**
**1 ounce Midori liqueur**

Fill a 14-ounce hurricane glass with ice. Add the rum and fruit juices, then float the Midori on top.

**Garnish with:**

1/4 slice of pineapple

1 orchid

# Sam's North Shore Smoothie

The orange and the cranberry juices mixed with the strawberry puree and the Grenadine syrup creates the perfect balance. The vodka takes it over the top!

Serves 1

1 ounce vodka
1 ounce orange juice
1 ounce cranberry juice
2 ounces strawberry purée
1 ounce Grenadine syrup
Ice

**Garnish:**
3 tablespoons whipped cream
1 maraschino cherry

Fill standard blender container 1/3 full of ice. Add liquid ingredients and blend. Pour mixture into a hurricane glass. Garnish with whipped cream and a maraschino cherry.

# Banana Fritters

The sweet, creamy texture of the banana is balanced by the crispy coating. The contrast makes this simple dish work. Bananas were one of the essential food plants that the early Polynesians brought with them to Hawai'i.

Serves 4

1-1/2 cups all-purpose flour
2 tablespoons sugar
1/2 teaspoon baking soda
1/2 teaspoon salt
1 egg
1 generous cup buttermilk
8 apple bananas, peeled and split
Oil for deep frying
1 cup granulated sugar for dredging fritters
1 teaspoon cinnamon
1/2 teaspoon ground nutmeg

Combine 1 cup of sugar, cinnamon, and nutmeg in a bowl, for dredging. Set aside.

Sift dry ingredients into a medium bowl. Combine egg and buttermilk, and stir into dry ingredients, mixing until well-combined. Place bananas carefully in batter. (They can rest in the batter, covered until you are ready to fry them.)

Heat the oil to 350 to 390 degrees or until the oil gives off a slight haze. Make sure bananas are well-coated with the batter before setting them in oil. Using a fork, place coated bananas in oil and fry for 2 to 4 minutes, or until golden brown. Remove from oil with tongs and drain on several layers of paper towels. Dredge drained fritters in sugar mixture and serve hot with ice cream.

# Lemon Pohā Scones

The lemon's tangy flavor adds a bright sparkle to the sweetness of the pohā berries. Fresh lemon juice and lemon rind with its pungent oils are essential to this well-flavored dessert. Fresh juices are far superior to frozen or bottled juices, which offer only compromised flavors.

Serves 6

1/2 cup pohā berries (cape gooseberry)
2 tablespoons lemon juice
1 teaspoon lemon rind
2 cups all-purpose flour
1 tablespoon baking powder
1/2 teaspoon salt
1/4 cup sugar
1/4 cup butter, softened
2 eggs, beaten separately
1/2 cup buttermilk

**Lemon Sugar Glaze:**
1/2 cup granulated sugar
4 tablespoons lemon juice

Mix dry ingredients and sugar, then cut in the soft butter. Combine 1 beaten egg and buttermilk. Mix until dough holds together. Add the lemon juice and lemon rind and mix until combined. Wrap the dough in plastic wrap and chill well.

Preheat the oven to 400 degrees. Divide the dough in half on a lightly floured board. Roll each half into a 3/4-inch thick circle, then score into 6 triangles. Place the two circles on a lightly greased cookie sheet and brush lightly with remaining beaten egg. Bake for 15 minutes.

**To prepare the Lemon Sugar Glaze:**
In a small saucepan, bring sugar and lemon juice to a boil, stirring to dissolve the sugar. Remove from heat.

As the scones cool, drizzle with lemon glaze.

**Variation:**
Any other berries or fruits

# glossary

**'Ahi:** The Hawaiian name for both yellowfin and big eye tuna. Often served in the Islands as sashimi (Japanese-style raw fish).

**Aku:** The Hawaiian name for skipjack tuna. Deep red in color and stronger tasting than 'ahi. Good broiled, grilled, or used raw in poke.

**Bean thread noodles:** Thin, transparent noodles made from ground mung beans often used in a variety of Asian dishes, usually added to soups.

**Bean sprouts:** Mung beans that have sprouted. Available fresh or canned.

**Breadfruit:** A bland, starchy vegetable widely used in the Pacific but difficult to get on the U.S. mainland. Substitute potatoes.

**Cilantro:** A pungent flat-leaf herb resembling parsley; also called fresh coriander or Chinese parsley.

**Chow mein noodles:** Chinese noodles generally made from wheat flour and eggs; sold dried or fresh.

**Chutney:** A spicy relish made with fruits, spices, and herbs. Often used as a condiment with curry or glaze for meat.

**Coconut:** The fruit of the coconut tree. It has a hard brown outer shell and when mature, the shell is lined with firm white "coconut meat." The liquid extracted from shredded coconut meat is used in cooking or for preparing various fruit drinks.

**Dashi:** A Japanese-style fish broth. It can be prepared by boiling shaved bonito flakes (buy them preshaved) or from a concentrate. Follow package directions to prepare.

**Enoki mushrooms:** A type of cooking mushroom often used in Asian cooking; has long, slender, white stems, with tiny caps with a mild, delicate flavor.

**Furikake:** A Japanese seaweed-based seasoning mix used as a condiment for rice.

**Ginger:** A brown, fibrous, knobby rhizome that keeps for long periods of time. To use, peel the brown skin and slice, chop, or purée.

**Guava:** A round tropical fruit with a yellow skin and pink inner flesh and many seeds. Grown commercially in Hawai'i. The purée or juice is available as a frozen concentrate. Guava can also be made into jams, jellies, and sauces.

**Haupia:** Hawaiian name given to coconut pudding eaten as is or often used for many coconut-flavored dessert.

**Hawaiian chili:** Small, hot, red chili pepper. Substitute Thai chilies or red pepper flakes.

**Hawaiian rock salt:** A coarse sea salt gathered in tidal pools after a storm or high tide. Hawaiians sometimes mix it with a red clay to make 'alaea salt. Substitute kosher salt.

**Hijiki:** A traditional Japanese brown sea vegetable rich in dietary fiber and essential minerals eaten as a garnish or side, or used as an ingredient.

**Hondashi:** Japanese fish broth powder.

**Kahuku prawns:** Farm-raised, freshwater prawns that are slightly sweeter than shrimp. Jumbo shrimp may be substituted.

**Kaiware sprouts:** Daikon radish sprouts.

**Kakimochi:** Rice crackers usually eaten as a type of Japanese snack. Also known as mochi crunch in Hawai'i.

**Kālua:** Usually refers to a whole pig cooked in an imu, or underground oven. Substitute turkey.

**Kamaboko:** A Japanese seafood product used mostly in Japanese soup or noodle dishes; also called fish cake.

**Kim chee:** A very spicy Korean vegetable pickle usually made with Chinese cabbage. Main seasonings are red chilies, garlic, ginger, and green onions.

**Laulau:** Pork, beef, salted fish, or taro leaves wrapped in ti leaves and cooked in an imu or steamed.

**Lemongrass:** Long greenish stalks with a pungent lemony flavor. Also called citronella. Substitute grated lemon zest.

**Liliko'i:** Hawaiian name for passion fruit.

**Limu:** Hawaiian name for seaweed.

**Lomilomi salmon:** A fresh-tasting Hawaiian salad of salt-cured salmon, onion, and tomato.

**Long rice:** Translucent thread-like noodles made from mung bean flour. Typically needs to be soaked in water before cooking.

**Lū'au:** A traditional Hawaiian feast that usually includes foods prepared in an imu, or underground oven.

**Lū'au leaves:** The young green tops of the taro root. Substitute fresh spinach.

**Lup cheong:** Slender, aromatic, dried pork sausages; also called Chinese sausage.

**Macadamia nut:** A rich, oily nut grown mostly on the Big Island of Hawai'i. Also called "mac nuts."

**Mahi mahi:** Also called dolphinfish; has a firm, pink flesh. Best fresh but often available frozen. A standard in island restaurants and markets. Substitute snapper, catfish, or halibut.

**Mango:** Gold and green tropical fruit available in many supermarkets. Available fresh June through September in Hawai'i.

**Miso:** A soybean paste made by salting and fermenting soybeans and rice. Shiro miso, or white miso, is the mildest of several different types. Available shrink-wrapped, and in cans and jars, in Asian markets. Can be stored for months in a refrigerator.

**Mochiko:** Japanese glutinous rice flour used in making pastries and some sauces.

**Ono:** Also called wahoo. Fish related to the mackerel. Best steamed, baked, or sautéed. Substitute monkfish or orange roughly.

**'Ōpakapaka:** A deep water marine fish found in the waters surrounding the Hawaiian Islands. Its sweet, delicate flesh ranges from white to pink in color; however, cooked 'ōpakapaka is always white. It can run from lean to fat, depending on the season (they're fattier in the winter).

**Panko:** A crispy, large-flaked Japanese bread crumb that adds more texture than ordinary bread crumbs. Found in Asian markets.

**Papaya:** A tropical fruit with yellow flesh, black seeds, and a perfumey scent. Other types may be larger or have pink flesh. The most common papaya in Hawai'i is solo papaya but all varieties are suitable for island recipes.

**Passion fruit:** Also called liliko'i in Hawaiian. The common variety found in Hawai'i is yellow with seeds and juicy pulp inside. Passion fruit juice concentrate can be found in the frozen juice section of some markets. Substitute orange juice concentrate.

**Pineapple:** A tropical fruit covered with prickly brown skin and topped with sharp pointed leaves. You can tell if it's ripe by pulling on a leaf. Leaves are easily plucked out of a ripe pineapple.

**Pohā:** Hawaiian name for cape gooseberry; a tangy sweet fruit usually made into jams, jellies, sauces, and desserts.

**Poke:** A traditional Hawaiian dish made of raw fish, Hawaiian salt, seaweed, and chilies.

**Portuguese sausage:** A spicy pork sausage seasoned with onions, garlic, and pepper. Can be mild or hot.

**Pūpū:** Hawaiian word meaning appetizer or snack to enjoy with drinks.

**Sake:** Clear Japanese rice wine. Other strong clear liquors such as tequila or vodka can be substituted.

**Sashimi:** A Japanese dish of sliced raw fish.

**Satay sauce:** A type of Southeast Asian barbecue sauce used to marinate meats.

**Scallion brushes:** Green onion stems that are slivered and spread.

**Shiitake mushroom:** The second most widely cultivated mushroom in the world. It is a medium to large umbrella-shaped mushroom. It has floppy tan to dark brown caps with edges that tend to roll under. Shiitakes have a woodsy, smoky flavor. Can be purchased fresh or dried in Asian groceries. To reconstitute the dried variety, soak in warm water for 30 minutes before using. Remove stems of both fresh and dried shiitakes.

**Soba noodles:** Japanese buckwheat noodles, thin, and light brown in color, and eaten warm or cold.

**Somen:** Very thin, white Japanese noodles made out of wheat flour. Usually served cold with a light flavored dipping broth.

**Soy sauce:** A dark salty liquid made from soybeans, flour, salt, and water. Dark soy sauce is stronger than light soy sauce. A staple in most Asian cuisines. Also called shoyu.

**Taro:** A starchy root of the taro, called kalo, is pounded to make poi. Its flavor is similar to artichokes or chestnuts. The leaves (lū'au) and stems (hāhā) are also used in cooking. Taro contains an irritating substance and must be cooked before any part of the plant can be eaten.

**Teriyaki sauce:** Japanese sauce or marinade with soy sauce, sugar, and fresh ginger—generally used for cooking meats, poultry, and fish.

**Ti leaves:** Leaves of the ti plant used to steam and bake fish and vegetables. Often called "Hawaiian aluminum foil." Substitute banana leaves, grape leaves, or corn husks. Available at wholesale floral shops.

**Tofu:** The Japanese name for soybean curd. Available fresh in Asian markets.

**Wahoo:** Another name for the ono fish.

**Wasabi:** Called Japanese horseradish, it comes in both powder and paste forms. Pale green in color and produces a sharp, tingling sensation in the palate.

**Won ton wrappers:** Thin sheets of noodle dough used to wrap food for frying or steaming.

# index

If you have any questions for Chef Sam Choy regarding the recipes, please write to him c/o Mutual Publishing:

1215 Center Street, Suite 210
Honolulu, Hawai'i 96816

info@mutualpublishing.com